Principles and Practice
of Weight and Strength Training

Principles and Practice
of Weight and Strength Training

Greg Weller

THE CROWOOD PRESS

First published in 2013 by
The Crowood Press Ltd
Ramsbury, Marlborough
Wiltshire SN8 2HR

www.crowood.com

British Library Cataloguing-in-Publication Data
A catalogue record for this book is available from the British
Library.

ISBN 978 1 84797 488 4

Acknowledgements
There are a few people deserving of a great deal of thanks
for helping with this book and none more so than Lianne, my
wonderful fiancée and expectant mother of our first child. Thank
you for being so understanding during the writing of this book and
for a great demo of a Sumo Dead Lift among others. Thanks to
my friends and colleagues Scott Stevens, Katie Mitchell and fellow
strength and conditioning coach Joe Rogers for their support and
help, and for agreeing to model for the pictures in this book. Last,
a big thank you to David Crottie, Mike Burt and Chris Gibson from
Body Reform Personal Training (bodyreformpt.co.uk) for allowing
me to use their excellent facilities at London's Canary Wharf for
the photographs in this book.

Readers may contact the author either via Crowood or directly at
gregwellersc@gmail.com

Designed and typeset by Guy Croton, Tonbridge, Kent

Printed and bound in Singapore by Craft Print International Ltd

CONTENTS

INTRODUCTION

The world of exercise has seen many changes in the last twenty years. Research has revealed a wealth of information, some of which has helped confirm certain training methods to be valid and consign others to be myth. Information continues to improve with the advancements made in sports science and in coaching. Research into performance enhancement is now more relevant and applicable to real sporting situations. The practical application of the research has also come a long way, with the work of some great strength and conditioning coaches all over the world turning theories into practice. Unfortunately, it is taking a long time for the effects of all this great work to filter down and some athletes are still woefully ill informed or badly advised. Athletes of all levels, from recreational runners to keen amateur athletes, and even elite-class athletes, still present with some very common yet easily corrected deficiencies in their training. With the collaboration of researches and coaches from around the world there is enough scientific and empirical evidence to allow for well-informed decisions to be made for their training and health.

Strength training is not just for sprinters, rugby players or weightlifters; whatever your sport or reason for exercising, you need to do some strength training. Runners of all kinds, from middle-distance to marathoners and beyond, will get better results and stay healthier with the addition of some strength work. All you footballers out there will benefit from some weight training; it could prolong your career too. Accelerating, stopping, changing direction and jumping all feature in the playing of football, tennis, cricket, hockey and many other popular sports. All these aspects will get better if you improve your strength and power.

One of the main objectives in training is the prevention of injury. If you are injured you cannot train or compete. Training must also enhance performance in some way. This means that training has to be made as safe and as effective as possible. Bear this in mind when selecting exercises for your programme and think about the associated risks against the possible benefits. Crazy balancing acts on stability balls with heavy weights, for example, are counterproductive and just plain dangerous. New fitness fads and training methods will come and go, but the big strong lifts and sound training principles will always be around because they work. Be wary of the latest over-hyped fitness fad and try to be analytical in your appraisal of it before jumping on the band wagon. This does not mean you should reject everything new; excellent innovations will continue to be made but they need to be distinguished from the gimmicks and fads.

This book will provide the information you need to look after yourself better and perform better. Even before you have built significant strength, simply improving your movement with some SMR and mobility work will make you feel better and improve your performance. Some athletes have set new personal best times after just two weeks by working at getting rid of trigger points and mobilizing stiff joints before they have even started proper strength training.

There are explanations on how to prepare yourself for training sessions and look after your body better, by reducing aches and pains and injuries and making yourself stronger and more robust. The first section looks at how good posture can influence performance by helping maintain muscle balance and joint alignment to allow optimal movement and expression of strength in diverse situations.

Next is the training preparation or warm-up phase, a progressive four-stage plan to make sure you are ready for your training session. Instead of ignoring your stiff back or shoulders and heading straight for the weights, spending ten to fifteen minutes working on mobility and stability will greatly improve your training.

Methods for strengthening and stabilizing the torso, or 'core' as it is also known, are explained and illustrated; some of these can be used as good pre-activation exercises as well.

The main section explains how to perform and develop technique for some of the best exercises for increasing whole-body strength and improving health and performance.

The final chapter on planning contains some example programmes and effective training methods to help you in your quest for strength.

CHAPTER I

POSTURE

Correct postural balance and strength are important for efficient movement in everyday life and for optimal performance in sporting situations and it all begins when we are babies. In the womb we develop in the foetal position and after birth we start strengthening the muscles that comprise the posterior chain. These are the muscles running from the head down the spine to the hips and down the back of the legs to the feet. Babies have great mobility and quickly start to develop the stability and strength they need to get to their feet and start walking. Motor patterns and movement are practised and perfected until they can stand, then walk and eventually run around with confidence and good posture. Toddlers have great squatting and dead-lifting technique too.

As children start attending school they find themselves sitting down for longer periods at a time, and this is when bad postural habits and muscle imbalances can start to develop. Kids need to move. Movement develops motor skills, maintains mobility and is vital to ensure healthy development of the whole body. As we get older the pressures of modern life make it harder to find opportunities to maintain optimal mobility and good posture. We spend more and more of our waking hours sitting down: on the way to work, on the train or in the car; at work for hours on end; on the way home again; and at home in the evening watching television. None of this is good for the posterior chain that developed so well in infancy. Then, to make things worse, because

we sit around so much we develop a paunch, so we start doing sit-ups in a vain attempt to get six-pack abs. This only adds to the overdevelopment of the anterior chain and contributes to poor posture, among other problems.

Athletes and non-athletes develop posture and movement dysfunctions through daily habits and poorly designed training programmes. Poor posture can lead to neck, shoulder, back, hip or knee and ankle pain, and possibly injury. Adopting the correct posture during athletic movements will reduce the risk of injury by making sure that all joints and structures are in the right position to absorb and generate forces. Good posture can be encouraged and reinforced with an appropriate mobility and strength programme that addresses muscle imbalances and movement dysfunctions.

Healthy Posture

Posture can be influenced by many factors, from repetitive sporting actions and frequently held positions at work or rest, to acute or chronic injuries, emotional stress and even sleep positions. It is a very complex subject and one that cannot be extensively explored here. Proper analysis and treatment of postural and movement dysfunction, especially in the presence of pain, requires the skills of an appropriately qualified therapist. However, some of the more common and basic dysfunctions can be assessed with

Side view of ideal posture: ear in line with shoulder, normal spinal curves, neutral pelvic position and alignment from hips through knees to ankles.

Front view of ideal posture: shoulders level, arms straight by the sides, pelvis level and alignment from hips through knees to ankles.

movement screens such as the Functional Movement Screen (FMS) devised by Gray Cook and helped with corrective exercise strategies. Below are some basic explanations of common postural dysfunctions, which will give an idea of how the body is linked through-out with many ways of integrating muscles for producing movement and providing support.

Healthy posture does not need to be perfect and the ideal posture should be used as a guide to assess where there may be areas that need attention. When the body is viewed from the side there should be alignment from the ear to the shoulder through the hip joint just behind the centre of the knee and down to the ankle. From the front the head should be held straight, the shoulders and hips should be level and, with the feet hip width apart,

there should be good alignment from hip to knee and ankle. With a good posture the spine has three natural curves: a lordosis at the neck and lumbar spine and a kyphosis at the thoracic spine.

Looking at static posture can provide some information of possible dysfunction, but it is also vital to assess dynamic posture. This is where the Functional Movement Screen is used to assess how the joints and segments move and interact with each other in order to perform effective and efficient movement. At the bottom of the squat for instance the pelvis must be able to tilt anteriorly, to maintain a strong and stable spine position. If the pelvis tilts posteriorly the lumbar spine will round out and be subjected to damaging compressive and shear forces.

Common Postural Dysfunctions

Rounded Shoulders

Some of the most common postural dysfunctions start with the position of the head. When the head is held forward of the shoulders it results in extension at the neck and a rounding of the shoulders and thoracic spine. The sternocleidomastoid is a muscle attaching at the skull behind the ears, running down to the clavicle (collar bone) and sternum, which exerts a simultaneous upward and downward force when the head is held in the right position. The downward force tilts the head backwards and the upward force tilts the head forwards. When in the correct postural position the sternocleidomastoid's upward force pulls on fascial connections running all the way down the front of the torso to the pubis, which lifts the chest and helps with the correct pelvic position. When the head is carried forward of the shoulders the sternocleidomastoid cannot exert its upward pull so the chest drops and the abdominals slacken, allowing the pelvis to tilt forward.

Slouched shoulders can cause neurogenic tension in the lumbar spine, which can then make an anterior pelvic tilt worse. In addition, the muscles across the chest, particularly the pectoralis minor, tend to be over-active and the muscles of the upper back tend to be under-active. All this contributes to what Janda termed the 'upper crossed syndrome' and is very commonly seen in today's largely sedentary population.

Anterior Pelvic Tilt

Another common problem is at the pelvis, independent or in conjunction with a forward head carriage. Anterior pelvic tilt is when the front of the pelvis tilts forwards, resulting in an exaggerated lumbar lordosis. There can be a number of contributing factors in any

Example of poor posture: forward head carriage, rounded upper back and shoulders. This posture can lead to neck, back and shoulder pain and movement dysfunctions.

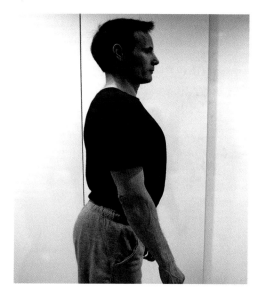

Example of anterior pelvic tilt, which can also accompany the rounded shoulder posture and can lead to back pain and movement dysfunctions.

postural dysfunction and it may be necessary to change daily habits or sports techniques as well as addressing mobility, stability and muscle imbalances. Anterior pelvic tilt can result in a tight lower back and hip flexors or a tight lower back and hip flexors can contribute to an anterior tilt. Rather than trying to discover what came first, the best approach might be to address the most common contributing factors. Sitting down for long periods can lead to reduced activation in the glutes and over-activation in the hip flexors. Repetitive short-range hip flexion, as in running and cycling, can also lead to tight hip flexors, which can then cause inhibition at the glutes. This is a powerful combination for producing an anterior pelvic tilt. The hamstrings attach to the pelvis and an anterior tilt will pull them tight, resulting in neurogenic tension here as well.

Such problems will result in inefficient biomechanics, which reduce performance, create fatigue and lead to over-use and acute injuries, not to mention the damaging compressive and shear forces that can occur in the spine.

Foot Pronation or Eversion

Foot pronation and eversion relate to slightly different foot movements that have come to be used interchangeably to describe roughly the same thing: rightly or wrongly, the problem is commonly termed 'flat feet'. Although some people may have structural flat feet, most difficulties are due to muscular or fascial problems, which can usually be treated and corrected with manual therapy techniques such as deep massage and addressing muscle imbalances. Over-pronation of the foot can lead to problems at the knee, hip, lower back or even higher up – for example, the right ankle has a strong relationship to the left shoulder. Conversely, hip and knee problems can lead to pronation of the foot. Either way, over-pronation of the foot can hinder performance and lead to chronic or acute injuries.

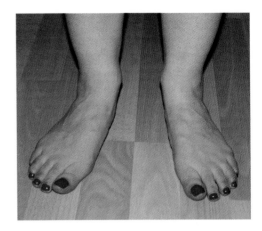

Over-pronated feet, with ankle joints not centred, feet turned out and arches flat. This can create problems at the knee, hip and back.

Pelvic and Spinal Awareness

The pelvis is an area worthy of special attention as it is the point where the legs and torso are connected and its position can exert an influence or be influenced by joints above and below. When there is an anterior tilt, the pelvis tilts forward in relation to the femur and causes the lumbar spine to arch excessively. In a posterior tilt, the pelvis tilts backwards

Anterior pelvic tilt: creates an excessive lumbar lordosis, which can lead to back pain and other postural dysfunctions.

relative to the femur and causes the lumbar spine to straighten out too much and appear flat. The neutral pelvis sits between these two extremes and should be the normal position for most people.

Posterior pelvic tilt: creates a flat lumbar spine, which can lead to problems with the spine.

Neutral pelvic position: the correct position for a relaxed standing posture.

Quadruped Spine Mobilizer

Quadruped exercises can be useful for helping establish pelvic and spinal awareness and may also be used as mobility/warm-up exercises. The quadruped start position is on your hands and knees with hands directly under your shoulders and knees under your hips and your spine in a neutral position. To help with spinal awareness, lift your spine up into an arch then lower your spine down into a curve. Do not go to the end ranges of movement; just get a little flexion and extension in the spine for a few repetitions, then return to neutral. Use a mirror at the beginning to help you get into a neutral position and guide the flexion extension movement, then try to feel when you are in a neutral position without a mirror.

Quadruped spinal mobility (neutral): starting position, with neutral spine.

Quadruped spinal mobility (flexion): quadruped position with flexed spine. Avoid going to the end range of motion.

Quadruped spinal mobility (extension): quadruped position with extended spine. Avoid going to the end range of motion.

Bird Dog

From the same quadruped position extend one leg back behind you until it is straight while simultaneously flexing the opposite shoulder until the arm is straight and both are parallel to the floor. Think about squeezing the glutes and gently bracing the abdominals to maintain stability while maintaining easy breathing. The spine and pelvis should not move. Hold this position for a few seconds and concentrate on maintaining a neutral spine and pelvis. Again, using a mirror can give good feedback.

Another good feedback mechanism is having someone place a broomstick or similar along the back. Keep the chin tucked in and neck in line with the spine and place the stick from the back of the head, between the shoulder blades and on to the pelvis. As you move the arm and leg keep the stick in touch with these three points and do not allow the space between the stick and the lumbar spine to change.

For more exercises that will help with posture, stability and awareness, see the mobility, pre-activation and core-strengthening sections.

Bird dog, start position: having the dowel in contact with the head, upper back and hips gives feedback on how to achieve the correct quadruped position.

Bird dog, finish position: maintain spine and pelvic position as you extend leg and flex opposite arm.

CHAPTER 2

TRAINING PREPARATION/ WARM-UP PHASE

An Effective Warm-Up

The warm-up phase of any exercise regime is vital to the effectiveness of the rest of the workout session. Sadly, it is all too often over-looked completely, or addressed with a few arm swings and a couple of static stretches. Some believe that sitting on a stationary bike or plodding on a treadmill for ten minutes constitutes a warm-up but it is nowhere near good enough. The body needs to be properly prepared for the demands of the intended exercise if we want to reduce the risk of injury and ensure the quality of the workout. If you are an athlete you need your workout sessions to be as productive and as safe as possible. The last thing you want is to waste time and risk injury with a 'junk' workout. The real skill in training is to optimize perfor-mance improvements with the least amount of training possible and implementing a full and proper warm-up is a vital component of an effective training session.

Think about the warm-up more in terms of it being the part of the training session where you work on mobility, stability and motor skills. It needs to be comprehensive and contain several elements that progress to movements specific to the upcoming training session. When you first start to implement some of these elements, take your time and get used to them as you would any new exer-cise or skill. Some may find the warm-up is the workout for the first few sessions. With prac-tice you will become more familiar with the techniques and your body will respond faster. Total time spent on the warm-up should be somewhere between ten and fifteen minutes, and possibly longer while first implementing new concepts.

The warm-up is comprised of four progres-sive stages that blend into one continuous preparation phase:

- Stage One: reducing muscle tension and density with a form of self-massage called self myofascial release (SMR).
- Stage Two: working on maintaining or increasing mobility in specific areas with targeted mobility drills and in multiple areas with whole body mobility drills.
- Stage Three: pre-activation work where the aim is to increase neural drive and excit-ability of particular muscles and movement patterns that are essential to all workouts.
- Stage Four: the specific warm-up. This is where the movement patterns specific to the upcoming workout are grooved to improve the execution of the exercises during the session and, consequently, the results from the training session.

A Note on Static Stretching

Routinely stretching the whole body prior to exercise is no longer considered necessary and does not constitute a warm-up. Static stretch-ing can definitely be beneficial for a muscle which is tight or short for some reason but it may also decrease force and power production and decrease coordination if performed prior to training. Tight muscles are often so due to neurogenic tension rather than structural changes and can be addressed with SMR and mobility work prior to training. This is more beneficial, as it helps to heighten neural excitement, prepare the joints for loading and warm the soft tissues, at the same time as moving them through increased ranges of motion. Muscles that are actually shortened due to structural changes such as a loss of sarcomeres and connective tissue changes may need to be lengthened through some static stretching as well. Otherwise, leave the static stretching for another time and only for muscles that actually need it.

The Four Stages of the Warm-Up

The warm-up needs to address biomechanical, physiological and neural factors to prepare for training or competition. The best way to familiarize yourself with a proper warm-up is to break it down into the four stages then eventually blend them together into a flowing, effective preparation phase that will address all the necessary factors.

Stage One: SMR (Self Myofascial Release)

Benefits of SMR
The first stage is to address tissue quality with some SMR techniques. SMR is a cheap, convenient and effective way of giving yourself a pre- and post-exercise massage. It does not replace a good, proper massage and if you are serious about your training a regular sports massage can really help. SMR techniques use a variety of simple equipment, from foam rollers to tennis and golf balls. The principle

involves using the piece of equipment to apply focused pressure to muscles and fascia. This facilitates the release of trigger points or tight areas through stimulation of mechanoreceptors. (Mechanoreceptors are neural receptors that lie in the skin, muscle and fascia throughout the body and which help regulate muscle tension and communicate information about the status of muscles and joints.) Knots or trigger points can occur for a number of reasons. They can be a result of maintaining a static posture for prolonged periods, such as sitting at a desk all day; they may also be caused by the repetitive movements that feature in many sports such as running, cycling or swimming. SMR should be done regularly to keep the knots at bay, or they will return and hinder your progress. The benefit of SMR is improved movement, increased blood flow and faster healing or recovery.

If they are ignored, knots or trigger points – areas of muscle or fascia that have become tight or gone into spasm – will become chronic and harder to resolve. They prevent the muscle from lengthening and shortening as it should and, consequently, affect the proper alignment and functioning of joints. The result is altered biomechanics, which can adversely affect performance and lead to excessive stress on structures, causing premature wear and tear and injury. Releasing these knots will allow for better movement and muscle contraction, which will give you better results from your strength training. This is not the only benefit. You will also reduce your risk of injury and heighten your skill acquisition from your training sessions.

When you first start to implement SMR you may find several tender areas that require a lot of attention in the first few days. After a while, when the worst areas have improved and you have got to know your body better, you may need to use SMR techniques only where they are really required.

SMR Technique

There are a couple of different techniques for SMR; you can try them both to see which suits you best, or you can use a mix of methods. One is to roll over a muscle until you find a tender spot, then pause and apply pressure on the tender area for about thirty seconds. Then move on to another tender spot and repeat the process over the whole muscle. Another method is to roll over a muscle until you find a sore spot, then move back and forth over the sore area ten to fifteen times. Then move on to another sore area and repeat. A third method is to roll up and down the length of the muscle without stopping. When you encounter a sore spot you just roll straight over it until you reach the end of the muscle, then roll back the other way straight over the sore spot again. It is rare for tender spots to disappear instantly with any of the methods and it usually takes a few days of SMR to get rid of the knots.

The best time to use SMR is still being researched and experimented with. It is undoubtedly beneficial before a training session, while after, as part of the cool-down, it can help with recovery and regeneration. Another possible application being explored at the moment is to roll during the rest periods between sets of exercises. This can help if you find you are experiencing tightness in your hip flexors or biceps femoris after a set of squats, for instance. Whether or not this is a good long-term practice is yet to be confirmed.

The Calf

A good way to go about implementing the SMR part of the warm-up is to start at the calf and work your way up. The calf can be done with a foam roller or tennis ball depending on how tender the trigger points are. Start with a foam roller and progress to the tennis ball (which is also a bit harder to use). Start sitting on the floor with your calf on the roller and using your arms for support with your hands on the floor behind you. Lift your hips off the floor and roll the calf up and down the roller. Target the bottom of the calf, the middle and at the top on the outside edge, which are the main areas for developing knots.

Calf: foam rolling for the calf, the most common spot for a trigger point is about half way up, where the soleus meets the gastrocnemius.

Fibularis: foam rolling for the fibularis on the outside of the lower leg; just below the knee is usually a site for trigger points.

Iliotibial Band (ITB)/
Tensor Fasciae Latae (TFL)

The ITB is a band of fascia running up the outside of the thigh connecting the peroneal muscles (down the outside of the calf) with the TFL and glutes. Start by lying on your right side with the roller at the top of the thigh and your upper body supported with your hands on the floor. Flex the left hip and knee to ninety degrees and place the foot on the floor. Keep your body straight, reach up with your hands and push yourself up along the roller with your left foot, keeping your right leg straight. Roll from the top of the thigh down to the outside of the knee and back up. From the same position, move the roller a little higher up to the top and side of the hip. Change your body angle slightly and agitate up and down this small area to try and find any tender spots.

ITB start: the ITB can be quite painful when you first try to foam roll it, so move up and down fairly quickly at first, starting at the top of the thigh.

ITB finish: push yourself up with your foot to roll down to the outside of the knee.

TFL/hip flexors: to target the TFL and hip flexors with the roller, start around the side of the hip and move round to the front where the hip flexes.

Glutes and Piriformis

Sit on the roller with knees bent to ninety degrees, feet on the floor and hands supporting your weight on the floor behind. Shift your weight on to your right glute and roll up and down. To progress this and target the piri-formis, place your right ankle on top of your left knee and reach across with your left hand to pull your right knee in a little. Roll this area, then move to the glute medius by shifting more to the right side and moving up to the top of the glute.

Glute max/piriformis: pulling the knee in towards you stretches the glute and piriformis, making the foam rolling more effective.

Glute medius: often a painful site, so move your hips round to the side and up and down to get the best result.

Adductors

These run up the inside of the thigh from the knee to the hip. Lie on your front with your weight on your elbows and the roller lying parallel to your right thigh. Lift the right leg out to the side and place it across the roller just above the knee. Roll up and down the adductors, close to the knee at first with small movements, then move the roller up towards the hip. Use small movements again.

Latisimus Dorsi

Start by lying on your right side with the foam roller underneath the area of your latisimus dorsi that forms the rear part of your right armpit. Use small up and down movements and try changing your body angle slightly to find any painful spots to work on. Moving your body back slightly on to the scapular can be useful.

Traps (Upper/Middle/Lower) and Rhomboids

Sit on the floor with knees bent to about ninety degrees and feet on the floor. Place the foam roller behind you on the floor and lie back with the roller across the upper back between the shoulder blades. Cross your arms in front and give yourself a hug to bring your shoulder blades apart. Then lift your hips off the floor and push your heels down so you can roll up and down between your shoulder blades. This area can also be worked on by standing and using a tennis ball against a wall. Make sure you do not press against the vertebrae and keep the tennis ball between the side of the spine and the scapular edge.

Pectorals

Lie on your front with the foam roller underneath the front part of your armpit, which is formed from the pectorals. Reach your arm out to the side and up slightly and start moving with small motions, changing the angle

Adductors: lie on your front and turn your hips into the floor to get more pressure on the adductors and move up and down a small section of the adductors at a time.

Latisimus dorsi (lats): foam rolling the lats can feel a little awkward so try rolling up and down a few inches, then move your body up the roller to get lower down the lats.

Traps (upper/middle/lower) and rhomboids: lie across roller and lift hips off the floor to place pressure on the upper back. This can be useful for relieving tension in this area.

21

Pectorals: stretch your arm out and change the angle as you roll up and down to find the tender spots.

of pressure to find the tender or sore spots, and work up and down for about ten to fifteen times. This area is best worked on with a tennis ball pressed in to the front armpit either lying on the floor or standing and pressing against a wall.

Rotator Cuff

This area can develop trigger points and tightness that can be best released by using a tennis ball. This can be quite a painful area at first and so just leaning on the ball might be enough to begin with, until your tolerance has increased. Start lying on your side with your right arm stretched out in front and the tennis ball placed underneath the area just behind and below your shoulder, on your scapular (shoulder blade). Move around a little until you find a sore spot and rest on there for about twenty to thirty seconds. One way to progress this is to start to roll around the area moving up to the rear deltoid and over to the latisimus and teres minor.

Another technique is a variation of Active Release Therapy where you apply pressure while contracting and relaxing the muscle. Flex the right arm to ninety degrees and start to rotate the arm internally and externally for about ten repetitions.

Rotator cuff: use a tennis ball or similar to get in deep to the rotator cuff muscles and rotate on top of it.

Stage Two: Mobility and Stability

Stage Two is mobility work. Mike Boyle and Gray Cook came up with a great way to look at the need for stability and mobility with the joint by joint approach. Starting at the ankle and moving up the body, it provides a simple way to determine where to mobilize and where to stabilize. The joint by joint approach is this: the ankle needs mobility (in the sagittal plane), the knee needs stability, hips need mobility (multi-planar), lumbar spine needs stability, thoracic spine needs mobility, scapula needs stability and gleno-humeral needs mobility. Clearly, there is an alternating need for mobility and stability as you work up the body. If the mobility or stability of one joint is compromised, this can have a knock-on effect on the joints above and below and lead to impaired performance injuries.

Mobility and stability can be reinforced and enhanced during this warm-up phase. Mobility drills use the contraction and relaxation of agonist and antagonist muscles to improve movement through enhanced neural control mechanisms such as reciprocal inhibition. Obviously, activating the nervous system and improving movement mechanics is of great benefit prior to training and will help enhance performance.

There are many exercises used for mobilizing different areas. To keep it simple, they are categorized here in to separate joint and whole-body mobility movements.

Ankle Mobility I

Stand up straight in front of a wall at arm's length and with the toes of one foot a couple of centimetres from the wall. Keep your heels on the floor as you bend the front knee to touch the wall and then return to the start. If that is easy, move your foot a little further back from the wall and repeat. When you reach the right distance from the wall you will feel a good stretch around the back of the ankle as you

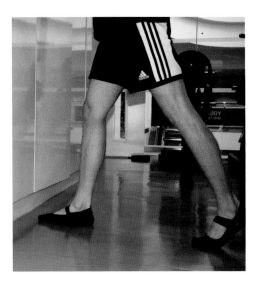

Ankle mobility I, start: start position with the front leg straight and foot flat on the floor.

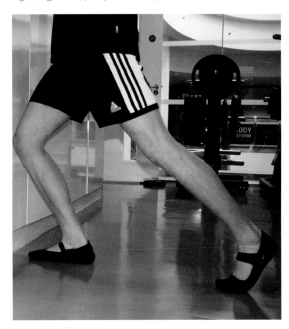

Ankle mobility I, continuation: keep the front heel down on the floor as you bend the knee towards the wall and back. Move the front foot further back if you do not feel a stretch in the front Achilles.

touch your knee to the wall. From this position touch your knee to the wall and back for ten repetitions, then swap feet and repeat with other ankle. Remember to keep your heels on the floor and do not allow the arch of your foot to collapse during the movement.

Another way is to touch the knee to the wall over your big toe for five reps, down the middle of the foot for five reps and over to the little toe for five reps.

Ankle Mobility 2

Stand nice and tall with the balls of both feet elevated four to five centimetres off the ground and heels on the floor. You might want to stand close to a wall to help with balance. Start with legs straight and bend at the knees as much as possible then return to standing straight and repeat for ten repetitions.

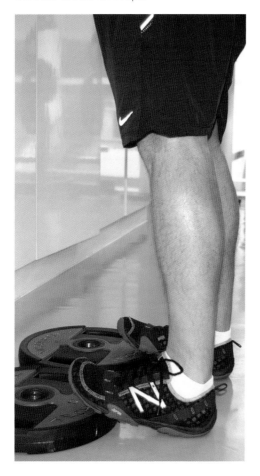

Ankle mobility 2, start: elevate the balls of the feet a couple of inches; weight plates are just about right.

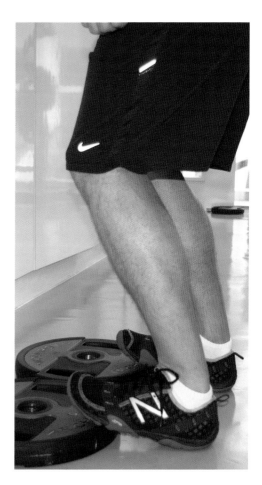

Ankle mobility 2, continuation: keep the heels on the floor as you bend the knees forwards and back.

Hip Mobility 1

Start kneeling in front of a wall at arm's length with one knee down and one up, and a ninety-degree angle at the knees. Tuck the toes of the rear foot under, keep the front foot flat on the floor and alignment from the down knee up through the hip and to the shoulder. From here, squeeze the glute on the down knee side and push the hips forward to get a stretch down the front of the thigh, then move back

to the start again. Keep the lumbar spine still and make sure the forward movement comes from the hip not from extending the lumbar spine or tilting the pelvis.

If this is comfortable, try reaching round and holding your rear foot up to your glute and then squeezing and moving the hip forward and back. This will give a bigger stretch to the rectus femoris down the front of the hips and thigh. Repeat for eight to ten reps each side.

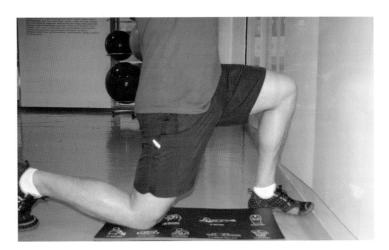

Hip mobility 1, start: start with the back foot on the floor and squeeze the glute as you push the hip forwards and back without extending the lumbar spine.

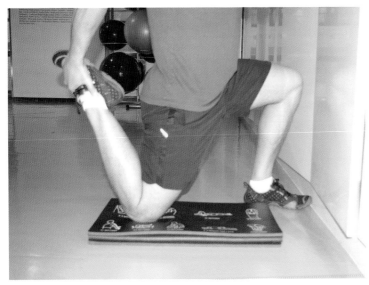

Hip mobility 1, progression: to increase the stretch for the hip flexors, hold the rear foot close to the glute and push hip forwards and back, without extending the lumbar spine.

Hip Mobility 2

Start by standing tall then take a big backward lunge step, bending the front leg so that the knee is over the mid part of the foot, and dropping the back knee to the floor. At the same time, flex the shoulders, keeping the arms straight, and reach up high. Squeeze the glute of the back leg and push the hip forward to get a stretch down the front of the hip, thigh and torso. Pause for a second, then push the front heel into the floor and return to the start position. Repeat on the other side. Keep alternating legs until total repetitions are complete.

Hip mobility 2, start: stand up straight.

Hip mobility 2, continuation: take a big step back and lift arms at the same time, squeeze glute of back leg and push hip forwards without extending lumbar spine then return to the start position.

Hip Mobility 3

This exercise targets the adductors by moving in and out of a stretch for the adductors that aid hip flexion and a stretch for the adductors that aid hip extension. Start this exercise in the quadruped position (see page 13)

with toes tucked under and back in a neutral position. Next, straighten the left leg out to the side and place the foot flat on the floor. Now rock forward and back, keeping the back flat and the pelvis in neutral.

Hip mobility 3 (adductors), start: place leg out to the side in line with the other knee and keep the foot flat on the floor.

Hip mobility 3 (adductors), middle position: try to maintain a neutral spine and pelvic position as you rock forwards and back from this position.

Hip Mobility 4

This targets the adductors from a standing position. Stand with feet about two to three times shoulder width apart. Shift the weight over to the left side by bending the left knee and flexing at the hip and keeping the right leg straight. Keep both feet flat on the floor and the back straight. Without standing back up, shift the weight over to the right side, bending the right knee and straightening the left leg at the same time. Keep moving from side to side for sixteen to twenty repetitions.

Thoracic 1

Good thoracic mobility is needed for efficient movement and should be worked on to increase or maintain a good range of movement. Start in the quadruped position (see page 13), with the right hand placed on the back of the head. Brace the abdominals slightly to help keep the hips still as you turn the right elbow and shoulder out to the side and around as far as possible. Turn your head at the same time so you look up to the ceiling, then bring the elbow back round to the start position and repeat.

Thoracic 2

Lie on your right hand side with knees together and bent to ninety degrees and arms stretched out in front with palms together. Keep knees together and in touch with the floor as you lift your left arm and turn it out behind until the back of your left hand touches the floor (if possible), then return to the start and repeat. Turn your head with your left arm so you look at your left hand throughout.

This one can be changed slightly to include a diagonal movement that also stretches out the pectoralis minor. This is a commonly tight muscle that can cause scapular dysfunction and lead to shoulder problems. Start in the same position described in the Thoracic 2 movement above. Move the hands down

Hip mobility 4 (standing adductors), start position: stand with feet about twice shoulder width apart, with knees bent a little. Move to one side, bending that knee and straightening the other.

Hip mobility 4 (standing adductors), continuation: keep low as you move your weight across to the other leg.

Thoracic 1 (side view): start in the quadruped position with one hand placed on the back of your head, then turn elbow out as far as you can.

Thoracic 1 (front view): keep the hips and lumbar spine still as you rotate from the upper back region, turn the elbow round as far as you can and look up to the ceiling.

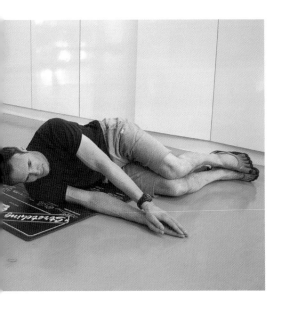

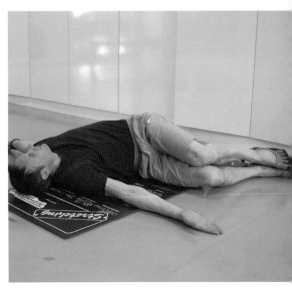

Thoracic 2, start position: keep the knees together, hips still and bottom arm flat on the floor as you lift your top arm and rotate from the upper back.

Thoracic 2, continuation: turn the thoracic spine as far as you can and try to get the shoulder blades and both arms down on the floor.

so they are touching the knees and keep the arms straight. Now lift the top hand and turn the arm over and behind you at an angle in line with the other arm, which remains flat on the floor. As you move the arm over and up, turn the shoulder and arm so that the thumb points down to the floor and get as much of the scapular and arm down on to the floor as you can. Remember to turn your head so as to look at the hand above and behind you. Keep the knees together and down on the floor and try to get the movement from the upper region of the back. Then return the arm to the starting position and repeat.

Thoracic 2 with pec minor, start position: arms are held together with hands down by knees. Keep hips still and knees together as you lift the top arm and rotate the thoracic spine.

Thoracic 2 with pec minor, finish position: turn the thoracic spine and reach up with the arm at an angle to create a diagonal line from fingertips to fingertips.

Thoracic 3

This one targets thoracic extension without rotation. Kneel down facing a wall about arm's length away with toes tucked under. Bend forwards from the hips and lean in towards the wall, placing the hands behind the head so that the elbows are lifted up resting against the wall in front. This is the start position. Keep your neck straight and lower back still as you push your chest forwards and extend the thoracic spine, then straighten to the start position and repeat for eight to ten repetitions.

Thoracic 3, start position: lean into a wall and lift elbows high. Place hands together behind the head and keep the spine straight with neck in line.

Thoracic 3, finish position: keep everything still except the thoracic spine. Push the chest forwards to get some extension in the upper back while keeping the rest of the spine still. Start with a small movement at first and concentrate on moving just the upper back area.

Squat Mobility

This movement drill comes from Gray Cook. It requires fairly good hamstring and hip mobility to perform properly so you may need to work up to it. Stand tall with feet shoulder width apart and knees slightly bent. Flex from the hips and reach down to grab your feet. Keep your arms straight and drop your hips down in to a deep squat, lifting your chest and looking straight ahead. Keep hold of your feet and straighten your legs as much as you can; you should feel a good stretch in your hamstrings. Lower back down in to the squat and repeat.

Progression for this mobility drill is to hold the bottom deep squat position while you lift one arm and reach it up and behind you, and keep the other hand on your toes. Turn your head and look towards the hand reaching up, then return and repeat the movement with the other arm. Keep hold of toes, lift hips up and go back to the deep squat position, then repeat.

CLOCKWISE, FROM TOP LEFT:

Squat mobility, start position: keep the knees slightly bent as you flex from the hips and reach down to grab your toes.

Squat mobility, bottom position: keep hold of your toes and pull yourself down into a deep squat, keeping arms straight and inside your knees. Lift chest and try to straighten spine. Keep hold of the toes as you lift the hips and return to the start position. Straighten legs with each lift to stretch out hamstrings.

Squat mobility, progression: in the bottom position, lift one arm, reach up and behind, then turn and extend the thoracic spine. Look up to the hand and keep the other arm straight. Pause, then repeat with other arm.

Press-up Squat

Start in the press-up position with the hands slightly behind and outside of the shoulders and the feet about shoulder width apart. Keep the hands on the floor as you shift your weight back, bending at the knees and hips. Keep the knees just off the floor and bend the hips as much as possible, then straighten the legs and lower the chest to the floor at the same time. Press up and repeat in a fluid movement.

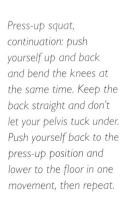

Press-up squat, start: start in the press-up position then lower down to the floor and stop when elbows are about ninety degrees and chest is off the floor. Keep body straight.

Press-up squat, continuation: push yourself up and back and bend the knees at the same time. Keep the back straight and don't let your pelvis tuck under. Push yourself back to the press-up position and lower to the floor in one movement, then repeat.

Combination 1

Start in a push-up position with the hands directly under the shoulders and the feet hip width apart. Flex the right hip and bring the right knee up, then place the right foot beside and outside the right hand. Drop the left knee to the floor then lift the right hand and turn the right arm and shoulder out and up towards the ceiling, turning your head to look up to your hand at the same time. Then bring the right arm back down, bend at the elbow and try to touch the elbow to the floor beside the right foot. Return to the push-up position and repeat with the other leg and arm.

Combination 1, start: start in the press-up position and bring one foot up to the outside of the same-side hand. Drop the other knee to the floor and keep the arms straight.

Combination 1, continuation: turn the arm and shoulder next to the bent knee out until the arms form a straight vertical line and look up to the ceiling.

Combination 1, middle position: bring arm and shoulder back round and drop the elbow down as close to the floor as possible.

Combination 1, finish: return to the press-up position and repeat with the other side.

Combination 2

This drill helps to separate hip flexion, extension stretch of the hamstrings (posterior chain) and hip flexors (anterior chain), all in one fluid movement. Start by standing tall then take a big step forwards, bending the knees so that the back knee touches the floor and the front knee is flexed to about ninety degrees. At the same time, bend at the hips and touch the hands down to the floor either side of the front foot. Keep the fingers in contact with the floor as you lift the hips by straightening the legs as much as possible, then lower the hips back down and touch the rear knee to the floor. Lift the arms straight up, reaching as high as you can while squeezing the glute of the rear leg and pushing the hip forwards. Now stand tall again and repeat on the other side by stepping forwards with the other leg.

Combination 2, start: stand up straight and take a big step forwards.

Combination 2, continuation: bend knees and flex from hips and back as you step forwards and place fingers on the floor beside the front foot.

Combination 2, middle position: keep fingers touching the floor as you lift your hips and straighten legs as much as possible, then lower back down.

Combination 2, finish: keep the back knee on the floor as you lift your arms, reach up high and push the hips forwards, pause, then stand and step through with other leg and repeat.

Combination 3

This one starts in the same way as Combo 2, but adds a rotational movement to the thoracic and shoulder area. Start by standing tall, then take a big step forwards and slightly to the outside with the right leg first, bending the knees so that the back knee touches the floor and the front knee is flexed to about ninety degrees. Simultaneously drop both hands to the floor inside of the right foot. Keep the right hand on the floor while turning the left arm and shoulder out and reaching up towards the ceiling. Turn your head to the left at the same time, so you are looking towards your hand. Return the left hand to the floor then stand and repeat leading with the left leg.

Combination 3, start: step forwards and place foot out to the side slightly, then flex hips and place hands on the floor beside the front foot.

Combination 3, continuation: keep inside hand on the floor and turn outside hand and arm out and up towards the ceiling. Try to get it in line with the stationary arm. Return hand to the floor, then stand, step through and repeat with other side.

Judo Press-Ups

This is a great press-up variation that includes some back extension mobility. Start in the press-up position with hands under shoulders and feet spread to about twice shoulder width. Lower your body to the floor keeping the elbows in close to the torso, then keep the hips on the floor and push the chest up as high as you can, arching your back. Pause, lower the chest down to the floor and then press up and back simultaneously.

Judo press-up, start: from the press-up position, with legs about twice shoulder width apart, lower towards the floor.

Judo press-up, continuation: drop hips to floor and squeeze glutes as you straighten your arms and lift your chest off the floor.

Judo press-up, finish: lower your chest back to the floor and push yourself back and up to finish with your arms straight and hips high in the air. Return to press-up position and repeat.

Stage Three: Pre-Activation

Stage Three involves activating movement patterns and important stabilizers that will be needed during the training session and comes after the mobility work. Mobility needs to be worked first to facilitate the activation of the stabilizers. Tight muscles and joints prevent the stabilizers from doing their job by taking over the role of stabilizing, which then prevents the main muscles from effectively performing their primary role of producing movement. Stability is worked during isometric and eccentric contractions so these movements need to be controlled and precise before being made faster and possibly explosive. These exercises are not meant to be exhausting so do not take them to fatigue. The hips, trunk and scapula humeral region are vital areas for targeted pre-activation as well as integrated whole-body stability activation and will be addressed in the accompanying exercises.

Quadruped exercises are a great place to start as they require stability from the hips, trunk and shoulders, all at the same time.

Quadruped Leg Extension

Start in the quadruped position of hands and knees on the floor with hands directly under shoulders and arms straight, knees under hips, toes tucked under and back held with normal thoracic and lumbar curves. Begin by straightening one leg backwards and lifting until it is straight and parallel to the floor, if this is possible. Think about using the glutes to extend the leg and hold it up, and brace the abdominals to maintain stability through the trunk. Hold this position for a couple of seconds, making sure your pelvis remains still and does not tilt or rotate. Keep the back still and do not allow the lumbar spine to extend. Slowly lower the leg back and repeat.

Quadruped leg extension: start on hands and knees and maintain neutral spine and pelvis as you extend one leg behind. Make sure you squeeze the glute to extend the leg and try to get it in line with the rest of the torso.

Quadruped Superman: start on hands and knees and lift one arm straight out in front as high as you can, without twisting the shoulders or moving the lumbar spine or pelvis.

Quadruped Superman

Start in the quadruped position and extend one leg as in the quadruped leg extension (see above), while simultaneously flexing the opposite shoulder until the arm is parallel to the floor. Again, do not allow any rotation or pelvis or back movement. Think about squeezing the glutes and bracing the abdominals to maintain stability and do not hold your breath; keep breathing easily. Pause in this position just for a second, then lower the arm and leg to the start without resting the knee or hand on the floor. Repeat the movement.

Side Plank/Plank/Side Plank

Start lying on the floor or mat on your right side with your elbow underneath your shoulder. The feet should be staggered, with the top (left) foot in front of the lower foot, and the legs should be kept straight. From this position, lift the hips until they are in line with the ankles and shoulders and maintain this alignment. Gently squeeze your glutes and push the hips forwards until they are aligned with the ankles and shoulders. Brace your abdominals while continuing to breathe easily. Place your free hand on the shoulder of the supporting arm and keep the shoulders down so the humerus is centred in the shoulder joint. Keep your neck in line with your spine, which should be held in the neutral position, and do not let the shoulders rotate forwards. Hold this position for ten to twenty seconds then move into the Prone Plank position with both elbows on the floor, feet shoulder width and alignment from the ankles through the hips to the shoulders. Keep breathing comfortably and hold this position for ten to twenty seconds, then move to the side plank on the left elbow and hold for ten to twenty seconds. Relax or repeat.

Plank/side plank/plank, start: start on your side with elbow under shoulder, body straight, feet apart and hips off the floor. Hold for ten seconds the turn into the front plank position without dropping the hips or knees.

Plank/side plank/plank, continuation: keep alignment from shoulders through hips to ankles and hold for ten seconds before turning on to the other elbow and holding for ten seconds.

Clams/Band Clams

Start lying on your side with your head supported on your hand, your torso straight and your knees bent to about ninety degrees with legs together. Keep the hips still and feet together as you lift the top knee up and out as far as you can, without allowing the hips to roll. Pause and lower back down slowly. Band Clams are performed in the same way but with the added resistance of a band around the knees.

Clams, start position: on your side with knees bent to about ninety degrees. Keep feet together and hips still and lift knee as high as possible.

Clams, finish position: try pressing a finger into the glute to help facilitate it and think about squeezing it. Pause for a second or two, lower back to start and repeat.

Band clams: place a mini band around the knees to provide some resistance and think about making the glutes do the work. Keep the hips still and torso still.

Bridge Lifts

This exercise helps to get the glutes and posterior chain firing. The glutes are the biggest muscle in the body and contribute to movement in several ways. They extend, abduct and externally rotate the femur as well as controlling internal femoral rotation and stabilizing the hip and pelvis. Without properly functioning glutes, problems can occur through movement dysfunctions and lead to injuries. These days people spend so much time sitting on their glutes that dysfunctions are all too common. Efficient running requires strong, well-functioning glutes to control femoral internal rotation when the foot strikes the floor then powerfully extend the hip to drive the athlete forwards.

Start by lying on your back with your feet flat on the floor and knees bent to forty-five degrees. Place your arms on the floor, keep your shoulders down and pull your shoulder blades together so they lie flat on the floor. Push your heels into the floor and squeeze your glutes as you lift the hips up until they are in line with your knees and shoulders. Hold for two seconds then lower back down under control and repeat.

Bridge lift, start: bend knees to about forty-five degrees, push heels into the floor and squeeze the glutes as you lift the hips.

Bridge lift, finish: try to relax hamstrings and lower back as you squeeze the glutes.
Stop when hips are level with shoulders and knees and do not extend the lumbar
spine. Keep the pelvis in neutral.

Single-Leg Bridge Lift

This version of the Bridge Lift is more challenging and provides more stimulation to the stabilizers of the hips. The start position is the same as for the Bridge Lift. From here, lift one foot off the floor and bring the knee towards the chest. Push the other heel down into the floor, squeeze the glute and lift the hips until they are aligned with the knee and shoulders. Pause, then lower and repeat.

Single-leg bridge lift, start: lift one foot off the floor and press the other heel down as you squeeze the glute and lift the hips.

Single-leg bridge lift, finish: keep the hips level as you lift off the floor. Do not let them rotate or drop on one side.

Bridge Walk

This bridge version activates the glutes by transferring the weight from one foot to the other. Again, the start position is the same as for the Bridge Lift. When you lift the hips, hold them up in line with the knees and shoulders.

Make sure you keep breathing while you lift one foot off the floor, hold for a count of two, then swap feet and hold for two again. Keep alternating the feet while keeping the hips in line and preventing any rotation of the hips or torso.

Bridge walk, start: start in the bridge position with hips aligned with shoulders and knees. Keeping glutes tight, lift one foot off the floor and straighten the leg, keeping thighs parallel.

Bridge walk, continuation: keeping hips high and level, return the foot to the floor and lift the other one. Hold for a couple of seconds, then swap and keep alternating legs.

Kneeling W to Y

This exercise is useful to promote stability through the hips and trunk and activate the muscles responsible for healthy scapular movement. Start in a kneeling position with the toes tucked under and the knees aligned through the hips up to the shoulders. Lift the hands and externally rotate the arms to form a big 'W' with the hands facing forwards. Pull your shoulder blades together, then straighten your arms up and out slightly to form a big 'Y' with your arms and body. At the same time, internally rotate your arms so that the thumbs point backwards. Keep your body straight, squeeze your glutes, brace your abdominals and keep your shoulders down. Pause at the top for a second, then return to the 'W' position and repeat.

Kneeling W to Y, start: squeeze glutes and keep knees, hips and shoulders aligned.
Start with arms in a W position and pull shoulder blades together.

Kneeling W to Y, continuation: keep torso straight while moving arms up to a big Y position and rotate arms in so that the thumbs point backwards. Try to feel the muscles between your shoulder blades working.

Prone W to Y

The above exercise can also be performed lying prone on the floor with the legs straight, keeping the chest on the floor and squeezing the glutes to help stabilize your spine and hips.

Do not lift your chest off the floor or it will turn into a back extension exercise. Keeping your neck in line with your spine, you should be looking down at the floor with the chin just off the ground.

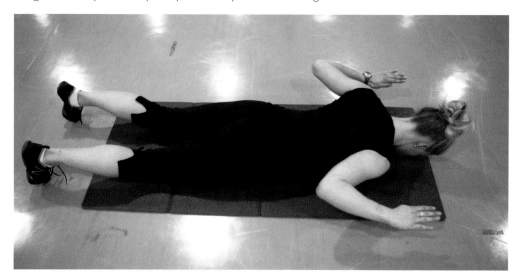

Prone W to Y, start: tuck your toes under and squeeze your glutes. Keep your chest on the floor, shoulders down, and lift your arms off the floor by squeezing your shoulder blades together.

Prone W to Y, finish: straighten your arms to a big Y position and turn thumbs up to the ceiling. Lift arms as high as possible, pause, then return to the W position and repeat.

Band Ls

A little equipment is needed for this one in the form of a resistance band or tube. It can also be done with a suspension training apparatus such as a TRX. This exercise targets the scapular retractors such as the middle and lower trapezius and rhomboids, the external rotators of the shoulder, as well as thoracic extension. This area is often overlooked, but it is important to work it as this will help to keep the shoulders functioning properly. Start standing tall, holding the ends of the band or tube in each hand at chest height, with the arms extended in front. Pull the ends of the band or tube towards you until your elbows are flexed to ninety degrees by your sides. Pull the shoulder blades together, keep the shoulders down and lift your chest. From here, pull the ends of the band out to the sides while keeping the elbows in at your sides. Try to contract the muscles around the shoulder blades to squeeze them together. Then return to the start and repeat.

Band Ls, start: keep body straight with elbows at the sides and hold a band in the hands.

Band Ls finish: keeping shoulders down and elbows in by your sides, squeeze your shoulder blades together and pull the band apart by externally rotating the shoulders as much as possible.

Reciprocal Shoulder

This is another great exercise for the shoulders used by Gray Cook to improve shoulder mobility and stability. Split kneel holding a secured resistance band or tube at arm's length in front at about chest height. Keep the down knee in line with the hips and shoulders and keep the arms straight as you flex the shoulder on the same side as the down knee and extend the other shoulder. Keep the shoulders down, chest up, and arms straight and slightly abducted. Retract the scapulars and hold for one to two seconds before slowly returning to the start and repeating. Do not allow the hips to move backwards or the torso to twist.

Reciprocal shoulder: start with arms straight in front of you, holding the band or tube. Keep the down knee, hip and shoulders aligned and squeeze the glute. Simultaneously flex the opposite shoulder from the flexed hip and extend the other shoulder.

Prone Thoracic Extension

Lie flat on your front with legs straight, hands under your chin and elbows out to the sides. Squeeze the glutes slightly to stabilize the hips and keep them on the floor. Look down at the floor so the neck is in line with the spine and then lift just the chest off the floor. The movement is small and only the upper part of your back around the shoulders blades should extend. Do not lift too high; the ribs should stay on the floor.

Prone thoracic extension, start: tuck toes under, squeeze glutes and rest chest and elbows on the floor.

Prone thoracic extension, finish: this is a small movement. Just lift the elbows and upper part of the chest off the floor. You should feel the area of the upper back contract and extend the thoracic spine.

Monster Side Walks

Resistance bands or tubes are needed for this one, a great glute activator. Stand up with a band positioned around the legs, just below the knees. Start with the feet hip width apart, knees slightly bent and the hips pushed back a little. Step sideways, placing the feet just wider than the shoulders and bending at the hips and knees a little. Do not let your knees collapse inwards, push the knees out against the band and keep the knees aligned with the middle toes. Then stand back up and bring the feet hip width apart again. Keep stepping sideways for ten to fifteen steps then return, leading with the other leg. Think about squeezing your glutes as you step sideways.

Monster side walks, start: stand with feet about hip width apart and knees and hips slightly bent. Squeeze glutes and keep chest up.

Monster side walks, continuation: step to one side just wider than shoulders, without rocking or lifting foot too high. Bring other foot in to regain hip width, repeat for ten to fifteen steps, then stop and return in the other direction.

Monster Forward/Backward Walk

Start with a resistance band around the legs just below the knees, feet about shoulder width apart and arms by the sides flexed to ninety degrees. Bend slightly at the knees and hips and take a small step forwards with the right foot, being sure to push out against the band. Keep the feet just wider than the shoulders and the knees in line with the toes. As the right foot goes forwards, the left shoulder also flexes and the right one extends. Then step forwards with the left foot and switch arms so that the right shoulder is flexed. Keep alternating the feet for ten to twenty steps, then stop and start stepping backwards. Make sure to keep the heels down as you step back, keep the knees pushed out and squeeze the glutes.

Monster forward/ backward walk, start: keep the feet shoulder width apart and the knees and hips slightly bent. The steps should be really small, just about a foot's length in font.

Monster forward/ backward walk, continuation: take small steps forwards for ten, then small steps back for ten, keeping the feet shoulder width apart the whole time.

Stage Four: Specific Activation

At Stage Four you groove the specific movements you are going to use in the main part of the workout. As an example, if you intend to work on improving squat strength you might start with body-weight squats or goblet squats, then move on to squats with just the bar and a couple of sets with increasing weight. After that, you should be ready to do your working sets.

CHAPTER 3

STRENGTH TRAINING

Why You Need to be Strong

To understand the importance of strength training you need only to look at how a certain amount of strength is required for just about everything you do. Getting up out of a chair, walking across the room, even standing still all need a level of strength. There are different types of strength and all are needed in some capacity by all of us. The exercises and training methods in this book are aimed at improving strength in a way to make you move more efficiently and effectively. The principles and practices used to train top athletes and keep them healthy are the same principles and practices that everyone should follow, although they should be appropriately adjusted to the individual.

'Strength training' to most people means bodybuilding-type training, using machines and free weights to try and isolate muscle groups with high-volume work in an attempt to get bigger. The truth is, bodybuilding training is for bodybuilders and most of us are not bodybuilders. Unfortunately, however, this approach has become so popular that even some elite athletes have misguidedly followed the principles. Elite athletes should not be training like bodybuilders. There are more efficient and effective ways of training to achieve sporting excellence. Getting stronger for most of us means being able to perform everyday tasks more easily, maintain a healthy weight, look and feel better, reduce injuries and perform better at sports and activities.

The right application of an effective strength-training methodology will achieve all this and more.

Benefits of Strength Training

For several decades much has been researched and written about the benefits of aerobic exercise while strength training has not received the attention it deserves. From a health perspective, strength training has been shown to increase bone mineral density, slow down and even reverse age-related muscle loss (sarcopenia), improve hormonal profile, strengthen the immune system, help prevent disease and stress-related disorders and reduce the risk of injury. Another valuable benefit is fat loss. Maintaining metabolically active muscle mass burns calories and an intense strength-training session can increase excess post-exercise oxygen consumption (EPOC) for more than forty-eight hours. EPOC is the amount of extra oxygen your body burns in the hours spent recovering from your workout and more oxygen consumption means more fat burned.

Getting older is something we are all going to have to deal with and research in this area has given us some vital information on how to reduce the impact it can have. Without the intervention of strength training our muscle mass starts declining from the age of about thirty. By the age of fifty, typical muscle loss is around 10 per cent and by age eighty the loss can be as much as 45 per cent. With such a significant loss in muscle mass, strength will decrease and everything you do will be much more of an effort. This loss is also linked with osteoporosis, heart disease, obesity and diabetes. The good news is that strength training can slow down the muscle loss and, more importantly, maintain high levels of strength into the later years. Maintenance of strength and power has an impact on injury prevention and quality of life and it is never too late to start. Eighty-year-olds have been shown to benefit from strength training, with increases in muscle mass, bone density, strength, power and endurance. Another positive effect is the impact on the endocrine system. Production of hormones such as testosterone and human growth hormone can decline markedly with age. Regular strength training boosts production of these and other hormones that help to combat the ageing process.

Bone density is also something that declines with age and can lead to osteoporosis, with potentially serious health implications. An estimated three million people in the UK suffer with osteoporosis, resulting in more than 230,000 bone fractures a year. Interestingly, some studies on runners have revealed that even they can have reduced bone density and muscle mass in their upper body when compared with sedentary individuals, suggesting that aerobic exercise alone is not enough for optimum health. Aerobic exercise has many health benefits and is an important part of keeping fit and healthy but, when it comes to preventing osteoporosis and sarcopenia, strength training is a must.

Aside from the health benefits, strength training is essential for anyone playing sports. Everyone, from recreational to elite level, from Sunday golfer to Olympic weightlifter, can benefit. Strength × speed = power, so a stronger athlete will have the potential to be more powerful and power is at the heart of almost every sporting activity. Stronger athletes will also be less likely to get injured and have greater work capacity. Understanding a bit more about how the body responds and adapts to different types of strength training may help clear up some widely held misconceptions.

If your main sport or activity involves a lot of aerobic exercise, then strength training will have another important benefit for you. It is well understood that aerobic exercise results in high levels of oxidative stress. Under normal conditions the body has an efficient mechanism for neutralizing this, through the production of specific enzymes. Repeated bouts of even moderate intensity exercise, for as little as twenty minutes a day for a few days, can result in oxidative stress accumulating to levels beyond the body's capacity to deal with it. This accumulated stress leads to high levels of free radicals that cause havoc to tissues throughout the body. Strength training has been shown to help combat this by stimulating the body's production of enzymes that mop up free radicals. This helps reduce the damaging side effects to health that can occur as a result of aerobic exercise. So if you are a runner, for example, you need to do some strength training for your health if nothing else.

Adaptations to Strength Training

Neural Adaptations
Most sports require high power outputs and many need good strength to weight or power to weight ratios. Boxing, wrestling, judo and any of the fighting sports, gymnastics, rowing, weightlifting, jumping and running – the list goes on. All these athletes want to get stronger but not necessarily bigger. You do not have to be big to be strong. The key to this lies in adaptations to the central nervous system (CNS). Strength increases are largely

due to inter- and intra-muscular coordination, which is the efficiency of the CNS to control movement and generate force.

Inter-Muscular Coordination

Very simply, this is the ability of the nervous system to organize and coordinate the activation of muscles into a sequence of contractions and co-contractions that improves efficiency of movement. The improvements in movement quality are the main reason beginners to weight training see early increases in strength. Better technique means more efficient control of movement, including stability around joints, which makes you stronger. Regular strength training will groove these motor patterns and improve the body's ability to generate force. One part of inter-muscular coordination is reciprocal inhibition.

Reciprocal Inhibition

This refers to the coordinated contraction and relaxation of agonist and antagonist muscles. An example of this can be seen with the muscles involved in the flexion and extension of the elbow, when the muscles at the front of the arm contracting the muscle at the back will relax enough to allow efficient movement. All movements require some co-contraction of muscles but being able to relax muscles quickly and reduce unnecessary co-contraction is one of the things that make athletes so fast and powerful. When sprinters are able to relax during a race they allow the constant contract–relax cycles to work more efficiently, thus enhancing performance. Reciprocal inhibition also plays a part in movement dysfunction. For instance, if the hip flexors are over-active they can inhibit the glutes, reducing their ability to function properly. The right strength training can improve the nervous system's control of muscular interaction.

Intra-Muscular Coordination

This is the coordinated activation of muscle fibres within a single muscle and consists of motor unit recruitment, rate coding and synchronization.

Muscle fibres are activated in bundles termed motor units. These vary in size from tens to thousands of fibres. The smaller units contain slow-twitch (ST) fibres and the larger, more powerful ones contain fast-twitch (FT) fibres. Between the ST and the largest FT fibres are several intermediate subcategories – Type I, Ic, IIc, IIac, IIa, IIax, IIx, usually summarized as ST Type I, FT Type IIa and IIx. ST fibres are smaller, and have slower contraction times and lower force capability than the larger, faster and more forceful FT fibres. Activation of these motor units starts with the smaller, slow-twitch units and progresses to the larger, higher-threshold, fast-twitch units as the demand for force increases (this is known as the size principle). The higher-threshold MUs are not recruited easily; it takes a very high neural drive, achieved through proper strength training, to activate them. This is one of the things that makes top athletes so powerful.

Again through strength training it is possible that the size principle can be overridden with selective recruitment of FT motor units by the nervous system (inverted recruitment pattern). Some explosive movements may cause an inhibition of low-threshold ST motor units in favour of high-threshold FT motor units, to result in faster force production.

Rate coding is the rate at which the CNS is able to send contraction signals to the motor units. As the demand for force production increases, the CNS sends more and more signals to contract and these signals build up until they reach a maximum level. An increase in rate coding means more signals can be sent and received, which means greater force can be produced. This increase can be achieved with the correct strength training.

Synchronization

The firing of motor units is usually asynchronous, meaning that they are fired in a staggered fashion to allow for a smoother movement. With strength training the nervous system can develop the ability to fire the motor units in a more synchronous fashion, which contributes to a greater and faster generation of force.

Golgi Tendon Organ (GTO) threshold
The GTO is a mechanoreceptor that monitors tension in the muscle and relays this information back to the CNS and spinal cord. If the tension in the muscle gets too high, the GTO sends signals to block further contraction, to avoid possible damage. As muscles get stronger, the threshold at which the GTO fires is increased, allowing for greater force production.

Muscle Spindle Activation
Muscle spindles, otherwise known as intrafusal muscle fibres, also act as mechanoreceptors. They lie along the length of the muscle and monitor the magnitude and speed of muscle lengthening. When a muscle is rapidly stretched these spindles send a signal to contract the muscle, to prevent overlengthening and possible injury (stretch reflex or myotatic reflex). In the legs this is a reactive response independent of cognitive processes. It is so fast it does not have time to go to the CNS and back; instead, it goes to the spinal cord. This reaction can be harnessed with the right training and, when combined with a voluntary concentric contraction, can generate very high and explosive muscular force.

Rate of Force Development (RFD)
RFD refers to the speed at which the muscles can generate force. Having great strength is not enough. You need to be able to use as much strength as you can in as short a time as possible. It takes about 0.4 seconds for a muscle to generate maximum force and this is far too slow for most sporting actions, which happen much more quickly than this. Ground contact time in sprinting is about 0.08–0.1 seconds and in throwing the shot it is 0.15–0.18, so, although increasing strength is important you also need to train for speed. An increase in strength allows for the possibility of an increase in RFD with the addition of appropriate speed training. In essence you turn strength gains into higher power outputs by implementing various strength-training techniques.

Morphological Adaptations

Increase in Muscle Cross-Sectional Area
Apart from all the neural adaptations another factor that improves strength is an increase in muscle size, or hypertrophy. Each muscle fibre is surrounded by a membrane called the sarcolemma, which contains sarcoplasm, the intracellular fluid, and myofibrils, the contractile proteins. Despite the large muscle mass displayed by some bodybuilders it is actually very difficult to stimulate muscle growth. Bodybuilders, as well as having the right genetics, train in a way that induces sarcoplasmic as well as some myofibrillar hypertrophy. This tends to be high-rep, high-volume training, usually 8–12 reps per exercise and 9–12 sets per muscle group. Lifting in this way means you cannot lift close to your maximum strength, which means most of the work is done by the intermediate type IIa muscle fibres and motor units. This makes it a form of high-intensity muscular endurance work and results in the muscle storing glycogen to supply energy for the workouts. It takes three molecules of water to store one molecule of glycogen. This is probably a large part of the increase in muscle size often referred to as sarcoplasmic hypertrophy, as well as an increase in non-contractile proteins, which do not provide any strength increase.

Myofibrillar hypertrophy is the increase in size of the contractile proteins actin and myosin. These proteins when activated are what produce muscle contraction and their size has a direct correlation to strength. Strength training with heavier loads and low volume will result in neural adaptations and functional hypertrophy of the myofibrils, without the unnecessary extra size and weight that are associated with increased sarcoplasm.

Fibre Type

Certain types of muscle fibres can be influenced through specific strength training. Fast-twitch fibres are bigger and have greater force capabilities than slow-twitch fibres. With the right training, some muscle fibres' characteristics can be shifted along the fibre type continuum towards the type IIax and IIx, to increase strength and power capability.

Fibre Type Alignment

The way in which muscle fibres are aligned can affect the production of force and speed and the type of strength training performed can affect the alignment of fibres. An increase in sarcomeres laid parallel to each other results in an increase in cross-sectional area and is associated with greater force production, whereas sarcomeres laid down in series are linked to greater speed and power capacity. Muscles angle of pennation can also be influenced by the type of training performed and this is another factor in the body's ability to generate force and speed.

Tendons, Ligaments, Fascia and Cartilage

All connective tissues are positively affected through strength training. These tissues are important for stabilizing joints, absorbing and transmitting forces and aiding efficient movement. Cartilage has no direct blood supply so it relies on oxygen and nutrients to be supplied through synovial fluid in the joint. Full-range joint movement is important to ensure that nutrients are supplied to the whole cartilage. When that movement is performed under load, cartilage can increase in thickness.

Tendons, ligaments and fascia adapt to strength training by increasing the number, size and density of collagen fibres that make up the bulk of these tissues. This increases their strength and, consequently, their ability to withstand greater loads and transmit greater forces. Because these tissues also have a poor blood supply, these adaptations take longer and this must be considered when planning a strength-training programme. Cartilage thickness increases with aerobic exercise as well as strength training, whereas tendons, ligaments and fascia need heavy loading to significantly increase strength and thickness.

Types of Strength

As you can see from the neural adaptations listed, if you are not doing any strength training you are missing out on something that could take you to a new level in your sport. Running is such a important component of so many sports that it provides a good example of how strength training can improve performance. Most runners already do too much running and very little, if any, strength training. Aerobic capacity is rarely the limiting factor and doing even more running is not going to improve performance. What they need is mobility and stability in the right areas, strength, power and, usually, improvements in technique. So, what types of strength are there and why do you need them?

Isometric Strength

Isometric strength is the generation of muscular force without a change in muscle length. Standing in front of a solid wall and trying to push it over is a good example of an isometric contraction – muscle tension is developed without movement about joints or any shortening or lengthening of muscles. Isometric strength is often overlooked and, although it should comprise only a small part of your training, it is still none the less an important and valuable component.

First, isometric contractions elicit a greater motor-unit and muscle-fibre activation than eccentric or concentric contractions. This means you can generate more tension in the muscle, which can lead to greater strength gains. However, because there is no movement involved, the carry-over of strength gains is mostly limited to around fifteen to twenty degrees either side of the joint angle used. This makes them very useful for strengthening at specific angles of weakness where a rapid increase in strength might be needed. However, not all angles are the same. Accentuated joint angles, such as those associated with a deep squat position or the top of a pull-up, can result in a carry-over of strength through the whole range of movement, although the further away from the joint angle, the lower the strength gain.

Isometric strength is also important for maintaining posture and stabilizing joints when prime movers are generating movement. It is during isometric and eccentric actions that the stabilizers are strengthened. Postural isometrics such as bridges and planks are great for helping develop postural control and strength. Isometric contractions are also great for teaching and strengthening postures during phases of lifts, such as the deep position in a squat or dead lift.

Isometric contractions can be held for various times depending on specificity and intensity. Sub-maximal postural isometrics where breathing can be maintained may be held for 30 seconds or more, whereas maximal efforts can be as little as 2 seconds.

Caution is needed when applying isometric contractions as they can develop very high blood pressures and should be considered only by healthy individuals.

Eccentric Strength

Eccentric strength, also called yielding strength, is the lengthening of a muscle under tension. The controlled descent during a squat involves an eccentric contraction and most weight-training exercises have an eccentric component.

A good way to look at the importance of eccentric strength is to consider the running action. Each time your foot hits the floor, muscles from your foot, right up your leg and into your hip and back, have to eccentrically contract to help absorb the ground reaction forces. During sprinting, these forces can represent as much as four times your body weight. Good eccentric strength will help reduce fatigue over the hundreds or thousands of foot strikes involved during a race and help maintain efficiency and good technique.

High levels of eccentric strength are also vital to multi-sprint sports requiring quick changes of direction. Having to accelerate hard and brake quickly can be very metabolically demanding and having the strength to cope with the deceleration forces and sudden changes of direction will improve speed of movement and resilience to injury and fatigue. It is needed when landing from a jump, slowing down the leg after kicking a ball or slowing the arm after throwing a punch. It is fundamental to human movement and should receive some training as a separate component.

Concentric Strength

This is what most people think of in relation to strength training and refers to overcoming a resistance with the active shortening of muscle. Concentric actions are present in most sports and activities – for example, standing up from a squat position involves the concentric part of the movement.

Maximum Strength

This is the greatest force that can be generated during a contraction. It can occur during a concentric, eccentric or isometric contraction and is usually expressed as a one repetition maximum (IRM) lift, or the maximum weight that can be lifted once. Most movements involve a combination of isometric, eccentric and concentric contractions and this combination is normally considered when talking about maximum strength gains. Increased maximum strength is fundamental to improvements in all other areas.

Relative Strength

This is the body's strength to weight ratio and is of great importance in many sports, from gymnastics to many of the track and field events in athletics. It is also significant in any sports in which weight categories are used, such as weightlifting and judo. Increasing strength without increasing weight can be achieved through neural adaptations to strength training. If you increase your relative strength you are going to find it easier to jump, accelerate, change direction and just about anything else you can think of because you have more strength to control the same mass. Increasing your strength relative to your mass will also improve your work capacity. For example, if you weigh 80kg and can squat with 160kg on your back, then squatting without that extra weight will be a lot easier and less fatiguing. In a sporting situation, this could enable you to perform repeated jumps for longer and to maintain a better level of performance.

Starting Strength

Starting strength is the ability to generate force at the beginning of a movement such as the start of an Olympic lift or the start of a sprint. Starting strength involves the generation of force with an initial isometric contraction, to build tension before commencing movement. Including some isometric strength training as part of your programme can help with developing your starting strength.

Explosive Strength

This is the ability to generate high forces very quickly and is expressed in a movement such as a squat jump, where the landing generates a pre-stretch in the leg muscles before a concentric contraction pushes you off the ground. Being strong initially will make you faster but you then need to develop that into explosive strength. Getting stronger is the foundation; you cannot develop explosive strength if you do not have the strength to develop. Obviously, being able to generate force rapidly is going to help you move faster, stop faster and hit harder, whatever you are doing.

Plyometric or Reactive Strength

Reactive strength is the utilization of the stretch shortening cycle (SSC) to produce a more forceful contraction. The SSC involves the interaction of the stretch reflex, stored elastic energy and a voluntary concentric contraction. Stepping off a bench then immediately rebounding off the floor into a jump is a plyometric action. Reactive strength training is a great way to turn strength gains into explosive power. To get the most out of this type of training requires a good level of isometric, eccentric and concentric strength, all of which are part of the whole SSC. Large forces are generated during reactive training and so a good foundation of strength is needed to cope with the stresses involved and to make use of them. Although high-level plyometrics are for more advanced trainees, low-level plyometrics can be very useful and beneficial to most trainees and can still provide improvements in neuromuscular coordination.

Strength Endurance

Strength endurance can be evident in an ability to perform repeated movements over a prolonged time; such as in running or cycling; a capacity for repeated explosive movements, such as sprints in rugby and football; or the ability to hold a static position for a given length of time. Strength training can increase the body's ability to perform repeated movements with less fatigue.

Strength-Speed and Speed-Strength

This is an important concept for athletes and refers to the continuum of activities requiring great strength with low to moderate speed and activities requiring great speed with moderate strength. Starting strength, explosive strength, reactive strength and strength endurance are all part of this continuum and most athletes need to work the full range, although the exact balance of strength and speed work depends on the sport and the individual.

Strength training has numerous benefits for everyone and should be a part of any programme for general health or sports performance enhancement. The exercises in this book will provide the basis for improving mobility, stability, movement quality and functional strength. Technique and quality of movement must always be paramount and weight and volume can be increased gradually as strength and capacity improve. Take the time to learn the movements correctly and seek expert advice if you experience any difficulties you cannot correct on your own.

Strength is a Skill

It is important to make the point that strength is a skill that has to be learned. Daniel Coyle's excellent book *The Talent Code* examines how talent is nurtured and the effort it takes to develop it. Talent it seems is not necessarily innate; it is something that can be learned, and he highlights the interesting point that, when people know a bit more about how they learn, their learning improves. Clearly, an explanation of how we develop skills should help us to achieve improvements in our own skills, including our strength.

On the physiological side of skill acquisition, myelin continues to be the subject of much research because of its discovered importance in developing motor control. Myelin is a sheath made of fatty acids and protein that wraps around neural circuits and insulates them, much in the same way as the outer covers of electrical cable provide insulation. This insulation speeds the rate of transmission of electrical impulses and makes them more accurate. The interesting thing as far as skill development is concerned is that the more a circuit is fired the more myelin wraps around it and further insulates it. The more insulation there is, the more accurate the signal becomes, and the faster the signals can travel. Clearly, repetition is a vital part of developing skill, improving the neural adaptations and getting stronger.

Equally important is the breaking down of complicated movements into smaller segments, and making mistakes. Learning movements in small segments makes it easier to identify mistakes and correct them before you add the next segment on top. It takes time to build the neural patterns and insulate them. Mistakes represent an opportunity for learning and building the correct patterns. Do not be afraid of making errors – go back a step and learn how to fix them and then try again. When you know you have performed something correctly, repeat it a few times then try the next stage of the movement, eventually putting all the stages together. Slowing down the movement will also help you spot the mistakes and correct them. Perfect and repeat the pattern with slow, controlled movements. When it is right, you can start to increase the speed.

Visual feedback can be a great help when trying to perfect a movement. Watch how a movement should be performed correctly at first and then visualize yourself executing perfect repetitions. This process of visualization and developing inner feel for the movement will trigger the neural firing and myelination before you even start to move. Use a mirror or video clip to get feedback on your own movement and see where you are making mistakes. You can then adjust the movement slowly and precisely and start to develop the correct feel. Developing awareness will help you to control your movements and build motor patterns. Start to think about how your muscles and joints feel, move and integrate.

When you become skilled in a movement, you can start to introduce variation. This will provide more options for the nervous system to react to and correct, which will improve the skill further and make it adaptable to different situations.

Do Not Train to Failure

This can be hard for some people to grasp. If you are used to pushing yourself to the limit and beyond with concepts such as forced reps, drop sets and pre-exhaust, to mention a few, you may find it tough to rein yourself in. If you need to use a spotter to help you lift the weight then the weight is too heavy or the reps are too high. A spotter should be there for safety only and not to help you lift the weight. What is the point of that? Pushing yourself to failure will induce neural fatigue, which will hinder your progress in both strength and skill. The earlier section on strength-training adaptations explains the importance of the nervous system in improving strength. Pushing yourself into neural fatigue will set you back and make all that hard work less productive. It can take up to five to six times longer for the nervous system to recover from an intense training session than the muscles; that means as long as ten to fifteen days, or more. Constantly pushing yourself into neural fatigue can over-stress the central nervous system, resulting in poor performance and, eventually, a decline in strength.

The best way to stimulate the CNS to achieve strength gains and avoid fatigue is to keep the overall volume down and get adequate rest between sets. For more on the correct volume and intensity, see pages 154–158 on planning and programming.

Train on Your Feet

What good is strength if you have to support yourself in a machine to use it? You need to be able to express your strength in challenging environments that require whole-body stability and control. Think about the sport you play, or just daily activities such as carrying shopping or running around with the kids. Everything you do requires a level of stability and training will make everything you do that little bit easier. Train mostly with free weights and doing exercises that require you to provide stability. Since we as humans have evolved to move around on our feet and most sports require us to generate force on our feet, it makes sense to perform exercises standing up. Standing single- and double-leg exercises will utilize the force transference link from the ground up the legs, through the hips and torso and up to the hands.

Keep Training Sessions Under an Hour

Making training sessions as productive as possible includes time management. Most people, unsurprisingly, are happy to hear they do not need to spend hours at a time in the gym to get results. Unless you are a full-time athlete you have to balance your training time with family, friend and work commitments. Keeping the training sessions under an hour will help prevent you getting burnt out physically and mentally, and actually improve your results. Training for too long may also be a contributing factor to neural fatigue. All these commitments add to daily stress, which can lead to elevated cortisol levels. These may also be elevated with long workouts. Cortisol is a catabolic hormone necessary during exercise as it is involved in the breakdown of glycogen and fat for energy. Unfortunately, it also breaks down muscle tissue and slows recovery if levels are too high, especially post training. High levels of cortisol will also eventually result in lowered levels of testosterone, which will affect your strength gains and recovery.

Fuzzy Training (Grey Areas)

One thing to remember is that, no matter how much research is done into how the body responds to exercise, there are always going to be anomalies. Research is done to isolate a particular response or adaptation in a controlled environment and, although the information gleaned is useful, it does not always work the same way in a real-life or sport situation. Nothing is black and white and there are always grey areas; this has been referred to by Mel Siff in *Supertraining* as 'fuzzy fitness'. There are too many variables in human performance to be able to isolate certain factors as being responsible. Everything we do relies on complex interactions between the body's many systems and there are many variables from day to day and between individuals. Relying on exact numbers to control training does not allow for variables and not everything will work for everyone the same way. Be prepared to change things if they are not working and learn to listen to your body.

How Strong Do You Need To Be?

The simple answer is 'stronger'. You do not need to be crazy strong or constantly push yourself to be stronger than everyone else you train or compete with, unless of course that is the purpose of your sport. In order to improve, you just need to be stronger than you were. If you start off being able to squat with forty kilos and after three months you are squatting with eighty kilos, your performance in whatever you do is going to improve. If you play football you will be able

to accelerate more quickly, decelerate more quickly, change direction more quickly and jump higher for longer. Rather than trying to be the strongest, it is better to be guided by making improvements first and then looking at strength to weight ratio.

To give you an idea of how strong you are you can use a percentage of body weight or a number of reps with body weight for a few select exercises:

[1]Squats and dead lifts

Squatting or dead-lifting with body weight – squatting with a weight equivalent to your body weight on your shoulders – is considered a good level of strength.

Squatting or dead-lifting with one and half times your body weight is considered very good strength.

Squatting or dead-lifting with twice your body weight is considered excellent strength. Squatting or dead-lifting with two and half or more times your body weight is considered elite-level strength.

[2]Pull-ups for men

Ten body-weight pull-ups is good.
Fifteen body-weight pull-ups is very good.
Twenty body-weight pull-ups is excellent.
Twenty-five or more pull-ups is elite strength.

[3]Pull-ups for women

Three body-weight pull-ups is good.
Five body-weight pull-ups is very good.
Ten body-weight pull-ups is excellent.
Fifteen or more pull-ups is elite.

[4]Press-ups for men

Twenty press-ups is good.
Thirty to thirty-five press-ups is very good.
Forty-five to fifty press-ups is excellent.
Fifty-five press-ups or more is elite.

[5]Press-ups for women

Ten press-ups is good.
Fifteen press-ups is very good.
Twenty to twenty-five press-ups is excellent.
Thirty or more press-ups is elite.

CHAPTER 4

THE TORSO OR 'CORE TRAINING'

The training of the core has been the subject of thorough research for a number of years and still provokes much debate and varying opinions. The determined pursuit of a six-pack can be witnessed in gyms the length and breadth of the country, but there is also a real lack of understanding of function and effective, safe training for this area. The work of Stuart McGill and others has helped enormously in our understanding of spinal health, core exercises and the role that the abdominals play in movement and in supporting the trunk and spine.

The most common exercises performed for the trunk are some form of abdominal curls or sit-ups, followed closely by rotational variations. This is where much of the debate has been focused in recent years. Should we be doing any of these movements – spinal flexion, extension and rotation – and, if so, how should we do them and how often?

In his book *Low Back Disorders*, McGill demonstrates that flexion of the lumbar spine generates high compression and shear loads and that repeated flexion can lead to intervertebral disc degeneration. This is obviously not a desirable outcome. So, does this mean we should never do sit-ups or ab curls? Not necessarily, but lumbar flexion resulting in high loads is hazardous and, as most ab curl variations involve lumbar flexion with high compression, maybe less potentially injurious alternatives should be sought. Even if prone spinal flexion is part of your sport, as it can be in MMA or judo, most of your abdominal strength training

can be done using alternative methods, saving your spine from excessive stress.

Comprising the core are the abdominal muscles – rectus abdominis, external oblique, internal oblique and transverse abdominis; the muscle groups of the back – longissimus, iliocostalis and multifidus, plus spinal rotators, as well as quadratus lumborum and latissimus dorsi. Although these muscles do indeed produce flexion, extension, rotation and lateral flexion of the spine, they are also involved in stabilization and force transference. Sometimes the hips are also included in discussions of the core – muscles of the hips include the glutes, hamstrings, hip flexors and adductors. In fact, the whole body is intricately connected to the core through fascial and muscular links.

Maintaining Posture and Stability

Maintenance of posture in static and dynamic situations is vital to injury prevention, efficient movement and the ability to absorb, generate and transfer forces. More recent research has highlighted the importance of being able to control and prevent movement around the spine, with a focus on preventing extension and rotation. Flexion and rotation occur mostly as a result of movement while on our feet. Running, jumping, throwing, lifting, you name it, most athletic endeavours are done on our feet and even those that are not still require training that is. As mentioned earlier, trying to generate force through a fully flexed spine not only carries a high risk of injury but it is also very inefficient and you will rarely if ever see anyone successfully attempt it. With this in mind, it makes sense to train the core with exercises to improve stability, but also to control extension and rotation and improve posture. Again, that pursuit of the six-pack has led to too much emphasis being placed on exercises lying on your back and repeatedly flexing the spine. Time and effort would be better spent utilizing exercises that help protect the spine and enhance performance at the same time.

Although strength is a factor in core training, it is not enough, and muscular endurance of the stabilizers is also needed if posture and stability are to be properly maintained. Do not be fooled in to believing that performing the big lifts such as squats and dead lifts is enough to strengthen the core and nothing further is needed. Strength will be addressed through exercises such as dead lifts, squats and Olympic lifts, but endurance, which is just as important, requires a different approach. Building strength through heavy lifts will improve core strength for bracing while performing a few reps but spinal stability also requires the co-activation of many muscles, to generate small forces over a prolonged period of time. Tempo is also important – when training for stability the eccentric movement needs to be slow and controlled. Isometric contractions are also effective for improving stability.

Abdominal Bracing

'Bracing' is the term used to describe the action needed to achieve and maintain support and stability for the spine. It involves the co-contraction of all the muscles of the core and should be trained through appro-priate exercises. Bracing should only be done to a level needed to achieve spinal support and stability for the activity being performed; all-out effort is not always necessary. This means that for most everyday low-level tasks the contraction needs to be only about ten per cent of maximal voluntary contraction (MVC). Too much contraction will lead to higher compression forces on the spine and wasted energy through unnecessary over-activation. It may also compromise movement quality.

The ability to brace while breathing heavily is also very important for athletes. The diaphragm and abdominals have to develop effective co-activation to perform simultaneous breathing, stability and force transference during sporting activities. This ability is not always present but it can be trained by performing plank variations during the rest periods of interval training sessions. Making sure the posture is good will promote the development of stabilization patterns while breathing heavily.

Exercises for the Core

Recruitment patterns for the core will differ depending on the situation, so a variety of exercises are needed to promote activation in different situations. The following exercises will provide enough variety and progressions to keep your core challenged and develop a strong, resilient centre of force transference and effective movement.

Floor Exercises

Prone Plank
This is a basic and very effective exercise for improving postural positioning and endurance. You must make sure you can get into the right position or the exercises may have a

Prone plank: elbows should be under shoulders and aligned with hips, knees and ankles. Maintain easy breathing and a neutral spine and pelvis.

detrimental effect. Get someone to observe you and give feedback, or use a mirror in the beginning to make sure you are in the right position. Do not make a habit of using a mirror, however; you need to improve your positional awareness without its help. It is important to learn to feel when you are in the right position, and practise achieving this without a mirror or help from another person. You will not be able to carry a mirror around all day to stop and check your posture.

Start by lying on your front on the floor or on a mat. Place your feet shoulder width apart and pull your toes up so that they are on the floor and ready for you to put your weight on them. Place your elbows on the floor under your shoulders. Now lift your body off the floor, holding your weight on your toes and your elbows. Brace your abs enough to hold your position while you continue to breathe, maintaining alignment through shoulders, hips, knees and ankles. Keep your legs straight, squeeze your glutes a little and try to hold a neutral pelvic and spine position. In the beginning hold this position for about ten seconds then lower the hips back to the floor and rest for five to ten seconds. Repeat for three to five repetitions. As you get stronger, you can start to hold for longer, eventually reaching maybe sixty seconds for two or three repeti-

tions with about thirty seconds rest between, still maintaining easy breathing.

Side Plank

The side plank position has a very different activation pattern from the prone plank. This position requires lateral postural stability from the ankle through the hips to the shoulders and places more emphasis on the obliques and quadratus lumborum in the core musculature.

Start lying on the floor or mat on your side with your elbow underneath your shoulder. The feet should be staggered, with the top foot in front of the lower foot and the legs should be kept straight. From this position, lift the hips until they are in line with the ankles and shoulders and maintain this alignment. Be aware of two common errors: dropping the hips too low and pushing the hips backwards so the body is flexed from the hips. To avoid the latter, gently squeeze your glutes and push the hips forwards until they are aligned with the ankles and shoulders; this should correct them. Brace your abdominals while continuing to breathe easily. Place your free hand on the shoulder of the supporting arm and keep the shoulders down so that the humerus is centred in the shoulder joint. Keep your neck in line with your spine, which should be held

Side plank: keep body straight and feet about shoulder width apart, with top foot in front.

in the neutral spine position, and do not let the shoulders rotate forwards. Hold for ten to fifteen seconds at first, rest five to ten, then repeat for three to five repetitions, eventually holding for thirty or forty seconds for three repetitions.

Plank with Knee Drops

This will teach you how to maintain a neutral spine and pelvic position and maintain stability while generating a flexion movement at the hips.

The starting position is the same as for the prone plank. While maintaining spinal position and hip–shoulder alignment, bend your knees and touch them to the floor then return to the start position and repeat for the required number of repetitions or set time. Do not let your hips move up and down and keep your shoulders down and your neck in line with your spine. Maintain the level of abdominal brace needed to keep stable and allow easy breathing at the same time. Start with ten to twenty repetitions and slowly increase to maybe fifty, as long as you can maintain perfect position and easy breathing.

Plank with Alternate Leg Lifts

This exercise teaches spinal stability and postural alignment while shifting weight from one leg to the other and preventing rotation at the same time. It also teaches single hip

Plank with knee drops: start in the prone plank position and drop the knees to the floor and up without stopping. Keep alignment between shoulders and hips and maintain neutral spine and pelvis.

71

Plank with alternate leg lifts: maintain prone plank position while you squeeze one glute and lift the leg off the floor a few inches, pause, then return and repeat with other leg.

extension without allowing anterior pelvic tilt and subsequent lumbar compression when done correctly.

Start in the same position as the prone plank, with abdominals braced and glutes gently squeezed just enough to maintain a good position. Lift one foot off the floor until it is in line with the torso; keep the leg straight and use the glutes to do the lifting. Keep the pelvis and torso still at all times with no dropping or rotation of the hips. Hold the foot off the floor for two to three seconds then lower it and repeat with the other leg. Maintain easy breathing throughout and keep alternating legs for the desired number of repetitions or set time. Aim for ten repetitions with perfect

control at first and slowly add repetitions until you can do forty or fifty.

Rotating Plank

Start in the prone plank position with the feet shoulder width apart, then turn into the side plank on your right elbow, maintaining pelvic and spine position. The feet should stay shoulder width apart and the body straight. Keep the neck in line with the spine, with the chin pulled in slightly, and maintain easy breathing. Hold for a couple of seconds then rotate back to the prone plank, hold for a couple of seconds then rotate to the side plank on the left elbow and hold again. Keep moving through the three stages for ten repetitions to one side then ten

Rotating plank, start: start in the prone plank position for a couple of seconds then turn to one side and hold the side plank for a couple of seconds.

Rotating plank, continuation: from the side plank position return to the prone plank, hold, then return to the side plank. Keep turning to the same side for ten, then do ten to the other side, or keep alternating sides for twenty repetitions.

to the other and add repetitions as you get stronger. Good control is needed to prevent rotation and maintain the correct pelvic position as you transition from front to side plank.

Hand Plank

The hand plank is essentially the same as the prone plank except the weight is supported on the hands with the arms straight. Most people find this version easier to perform as gravity cannot apply as much force on the body as in the prone plank due to the higher angle. Maintaining correct posture also seems to be easier. The advantage is it provides a great starting position for a variety of exercises and stability work for the shoulders.

Keep the legs straight with feet hip width apart and maintain a neutral pelvis and spine.

Hand plank: keep arms straight and directly under shoulders. Maintain neutral spine and pelvis and alignment from shoulders through hips to knees and ankles.

Hand plank with alternate shoulder touch: start in the hand plank position and brace your abdominals harder to prevent the hips rotating as you lift one hand and touch it to your shoulder.

Hands should be shoulder width apart and directly under the shoulders. Keep breathing easily while holding this position for the desired time. Maintain shoulder, hip, knee and ankle alignment and do not allow the shoulders to shrug up. Start holding for ten to fifteen seconds and build up to sixty seconds.

Hand Plank with Alternate Shoulder Touch

This development from the hand plank involves taking one hand off the floor and touching it to the opposite shoulder before placing it back on the floor. The weight shift forces stabilization through the supporting shoulder as well as the trunk and hips. You will need to brace the abdominals harder as you lift your hand off the floor, to prevent your hips rotating, and then relax a little when your hand returns to the floor. Practise this relax–contract cycle as you alternate hands but maintain enough brace to hold a perfect position.

Hand Plank with Alternate Hip Flexion

Start in the hand plank position and maintain posture and easy breathing while flexing one hip as high as possible without altering the pelvic or spinal position. Without compromising hip and trunk posture, alternate hip flexion for the desired number of repetitions or time. Do not allow the shoulders to shrug up or the back to round when flexing the hip. Start with ten to twenty alternating repetitions and gradually increase to a level of forty or fifty, without loss of form.

Hand plank with alternate hip flexion: maintain neutral spine and pelvis while you flex one hip as much as you can without twisting or dropping the hips.

Hand Plank with Alternate Leg Lifts

To perform this variation start in the hand plank position and maintain your posture and easy breathing while lifting one foot off the floor. Maintain alignment from the ankles right through the hips to the shoulders and neck. Gently brace the abdominals and breathe easily while using the glutes to lift one leg off the floor. Keep the leg straight and only lift it as high as you can without tilting the pelvis or moving the back. Control the rotational forces and do not allow the hips to drop or twist; use increased bracing to maintain form.

Hand plank with alternate leg lift: maintain neutral spine and pelvis while squeezing the glutes and lifting one leg a few inches. Do not lift hips out of alignment with shoulders and knees or allow any rotation.

Hand Plank with Hip Flexion Extension

This version puts the previous two movements together to perform a cyclical movement of the hips while keeping the pelvis and back still. First, lift one leg off the floor, making sure to use the glute to extend the hip, then flex the hip and knee without touching the foot to the floor. Flex the hip and knee as much as possible while keeping the pelvis and back still. Pause for a second then return to the start position and repeat with the other leg. Concentrate on perfect technique rather than performing high repetitions; start with ten and work up to twenty or thirty.

Hand plank with hip flexion extension: start in the hand plank position with neutral spine and pelvis.

Hand plank with hip flexion extension, start: squeeze glute and lift one leg a few inches off the floor, keeping hips and spine still. Pause for one second, then flex the hip and knee.

Hand plank with hip flexion extension, continuation: keep the foot off the floor as you flex the hip and knee and keep the back and pelvis still, then straighten the leg back out and return the foot to the floor. Repeat with other leg and keep alternating.

Stability Ball Exercises

Big inflatable balls have been used for years in rehabilitation and exercise settings and, when used appropriately, they can be a great addition to any exercise programme. Unfortunately, some people are tempted to do all kinds of crazy stunts with them, in the misguided belief that they are improving their performance. Remember, exercises should always be evaluated according to their risk and benefit. Standing on a stability ball and attempting to squat or press a weight is both pointless and very dangerous.

Stability balls are best used to add another challenge to trunk and shoulder stability with some simple but effective exercises.

Ball Planks

Some of the plank exercises can be performed in the same way as they are on the floor, but with the elbows or hands placed on a stability ball instead. Prone plank, hand plank, plank with knee flexion, plank with leg lifts, plank with hip flexion extension, can all be performed on a stability ball and this will provide a different challenge to trunk stability.

The Ball Saw

This exercise is great for developing control of spinal extension and getting some scapular movement going. The starting position is the plank, with the elbows on the ball. Hold the body still while moving the elbows forwards of the shoulders and back to the start. Only move the elbows as far forwards as you can while keeping the spine still and not allowing any extension or pelvic tilt. As the elbows move forwards you should feel the abdominals brace more, in response to the increased load. Do not hold your breath during the exercise, but maintain regular breathing. Start with just a few repetitions to get the feel for controlling the spinal extension and increase endurance by gradually working up to forty or fifty repetitions.

Ball plank: stability balls are great for improving co-activation of the torso muscles. Start kneeling on the floor with elbows on the ball, then lift knees and maintain a straight line from shoulders through hips, knees and ankles.

Ball saw, start: this is great for controlling spinal extension. Start in the ball plank position with elbows under shoulders and chest off the ball.

Ball saw, continuation: hold the body straight and still as you move the elbows forwards a couple of inches and back again. Keep the movement small until you get stronger. Do not allow your hips to drop or the back to sag.

Stirring the Pot

This exercise, one of the advanced exercises recommended by Stuart McGill, forces activation patterns to constantly shift by moving the elbows in a circular motion while balancing on a stability ball. The start is again in the plank position with the elbows on the ball and the feet about shoulder width apart to help maintain stability. Move the elbows out to the left then forwards out to the right and back, creating a circular movement. Repeat or stop and alternate directions for desired repetitions. Try ten to one side followed by ten to the other, or twenty alternating repetitions.

From the list of exercises all kinds of combinations can be put together. For example try doing ten repetitions of alternating hip flexion followed by ten repetitions of the saw without a break.

Stirring the Pot, start: starting with the plank position on the ball, keep body straight and still as you move the elbows out to one side, round to the front, over to the other side and back to the start.

Stirring the Pot, continuation: perform circles with the elbows in the same direction for ten repetitions, then change direction, or change direction with every repetition.

Roll-Outs

Roll-outs strengthen the abdominals in one of their major functions, which is preventing spinal extension. The following roll-out exercises will give a useful progression to work through.

Kneeling Stability Ball Roll-Outs

Start by kneeling on the floor with the hands on a stability ball in front of you. Keep the body straight from the knees through the hips to the shoulders and keep the arms straight. Start to roll the ball forwards, keeping the body and arms straight. Allow the ball to roll up the forearms as far as you can without allowing any movement from the spine or pelvis and ensuring that you can maintain the spine and pelvic position when returning to the start position. When you first try this, be careful not to roll out too far and cause your lumbar spine to extend.

Kneeling stability ball roll-outs, start: keep the alignment from knees through hips to the shoulders as you start to roll the ball forwards.

Kneeling stability ball roll-outs, continuation: stop when your elbows are on the ball and return to the start position keeping the alignment from shoulders to knees throught.

Kneeling stability ball roll-outs, progression: as you get stronger, roll the ball further out until your arms are straight.

Kneeling Olympic Bar Roll-Outs

This is harder than on a stability ball because the bar stays in your hands and thus creates a much longer lever. This allows you to get closer to the floor, which allows greater gravitational forces to act on your body.

First, put a couple of small, 5- or 10-kg bumper plates on the bar, then kneel with your body straight from knees to ears and hold the Olympic bar in your hands. The arms should be kept straight with the hands directly under the shoulders. Slowly roll the bar forwards just a little at first then return to the start position. Try to roll out further, as far as you can with good control and still being able to return to the start. This is a hard exercise so increase repetitions slowly. If you can perform ten repetitions without rest you are doing well.

CLOCKWISE FROM TOP LEFT: *Kneeling Olympic bar roll-outs, start: start with your arms straight and perpendicular to the floor and alignment from shoulders through hips to knees.*

Kneeling Olympic bar roll-outs, continuation: maintain a neutral spine and pelvis as you start to roll the bar forwards. Just move a small distance at first and make sure you can return to the start position without losing spine or pelvic position.

Kneeling Olympic bar roll-outs, progression: as you get stronger, roll the bar further out until you can touch your nose to the floor and return without loss of technique.

Cable Exercises

Adjustable cables are great versatile pieces of kit and have been used to develop chopping and lifting exercises to target trunk stability. Both Gray Cook and Mike Boyle have used cables extensively for years in kneeling, half-kneeling and standing positions to successfully develop core function. The different positions, from kneeling to standing, challenge trunk stability in various ways. Tall kneeling provides a greater challenge in the sagittal plane as does standing tall, while half-kneeling and split standing provide more of a frontal-plane challenge. All variations are also great for stabilizing in the transverse plane.

Half-Kneeling Cable Lift

The half-kneeling lift and chop are mainly for improving stability through the hips and torso. Keep relaxed while performing these exercises and breathe comfortably while gently bracing the abdominals when needed. Do not hold your breath or constantly brace and tense your body.

Start in a half-kneeling position perpendicular to a cable with ninety degrees at the knees and the inside knee down on the floor. Set the cable down at the floor and hold the cable with straight arms down by the inside hip. Keep the torso straight and the hip in line with the knee as you pull the cable up to your chest and then push it up and out over the opposite shoulder. Pause then return to the start and repeat. Try to keep your body still throughout and you may well feel quite a bit of stability work going on through the inside hip.

ABOVE RIGHT: *Half-kneeling cable lift, start: make sure the down knee is inside, next to the cable and the handle is held by the thigh. Set hip in line with shoulder and knee and look straight ahead.*

RIGHT: *Half-kneeling cable lift, continuation: maintain shoulder, hip and knee alignment as you pull with the outside arm and push with the inside arm and bring the handle to your chest.*

Half-kneeling cable lift, finish: keep your hips in line and your chest up as you push the handle away from the cable machine and straighten the inside arm, then pause and lower back under control.

Half-Kneeling Cable Chop

For the chop you need to set the cable position high up on the column and have the outside knee down on the floor and the inside knee up with the foot flat on the floor. Keep ninety degrees at the knees, chest up and torso straight. Hold the handle with a supinated grip with the inside hand and place the outside hand on top. The inside arm will be bent to about ninety degrees to start and the outside arm will be almost straight and reaching across your chest. Keep your hips and lower back still as you pull the handle into your chest and then push it down towards the outside of your down hip. Keep the hips still and only allow a little rotation from the thoracic spine as you turn the shoulders slightly when pushing the cable down to your hip.

CLOCKWISE FROM TOP LEFT:

Half-kneeling cable chop, start: set the handle a little above head height and start with the down knee on the outside from the cable. Get the hips in line with the shoulders and knee and keep the chest facing forwards.

Half-kneeling cable chop, continuation: maintain shoulder hip and knee alignment as you pull the handle into your chest. Do not allow any flexion from the torso.

Half-kneeling cable chop, finish: keep hips in line and torso straight as you press the cable down to the front of the outside thigh. The shoulders and upper back can rotate slightly but do not flex the spine or hips. Return the handle under control to the start.

Standing Cable Lift

The standing lift and chop provide an opportunity to challenge hip and torso stability and strength in a standing position. The transference of forces from the feet up though the body to the hands makes these great exercises for sports preparation. Done correctly, they will also reinforce the concept of generating rotation from the hips and thoracic spine while maintaining stability in the lumbar spine.

Set the cable at the lowest position and hold the handle in both hands, standing a couple of feet back with arms straight. Stand with feet about shoulder width apart, at a slight angle to the cable column and slightly bent at the knees and waist. Start with the inside foot flat on the floor and the outside foot on the toes; most of the weight will be on the inside leg. Push the inside foot into the floor and pull the handle to the chest at the same time. As you do this, shift the weight to both feet with both heels on the ground. Then shift the weight to the outside foot, lift on to the toes of the inside foot, turn the hips away from the cable column and press the handle up in a diagonal from the start position. Reverse the movement back to the start position and repeat.

This exercise can be changed slightly by keeping the arms straight, to create a longer lever, and then turning in the same way. This will take the pull and push part out of the movement and so present a different challenge to the core.

Standing cable lift, start: stand just behind and at a slight angle to the cable and hold the handle with arms straight and knees slightly bent.

Standing cable lift, continuation: in one smooth move, pull the handle to your chest, turn your hips away from the cable and press the handle up in a diagonal movement. Keep the torso straight and turn from the hips.

Standing Cable Chop

Set the cable to the highest setting and stand up straight, side on to the cable column a couple of feet away. Start with the feet just wider than shoulder width apart and turn towards the cable column by rotating at the hips and lifting the heel of the outside foot. Hold the handle just above head height in both hands and pull it down in to the chest as you turn the hips out. Then push the handle down as you shift your weight to the outside leg and lift the inside heel while turning the hip. All this should be done as one continuous smooth motion with rotation coming from the hips and shoulders and not the lumbar spine.

Standing cable chop, start: stand just behind and at a slight angle to the cable with hands a little higher than your head and knees slightly bent.

Standing cable chop, continuation: pull the handle down to the middle of your torso, turn your hips and press the handle down in one continuous movement. Do not flex the torso and return under control, turning the hips back toward the cable.

Half-Kneeling Pallof Press

Named after physical therapist John Pallof, these exercises can be done in a kneeling or standing position and are excellent for teaching rotational control.

For the half-kneeling Pallof press, start half-kneeling perpendicular to the cable, holding the handle with both hands in at the centre of the chest. Knees should be bent to ninety degrees with the inside knee down and the outside knee up. Keep the shoulders down and maintain alignment from the down knee through the hip up to the shoulder and the ear. Stay relaxed and press the hands forwards until the arms are straight and the handle is directly in line with your sternum. You should feel the abdominals brace harder as you move the hands further forwards. Pause in this position for two to three seconds, then return to the start and allow the abdominals to relax. Think about pulling the shoulder blades together when the handle is at your chest and pulling them apart when you press the handle forwards. Remember to breathe easily.

Half-kneeling Pallof press, start: half-kneel with down knee inside and cable set level with your chest. Start with the handle held in at the chest, with shoulders down and down hip in line with shoulders and knee.

Half-kneeling Pallof press, continuation: keep shoulders down and torso straight and maintain hip alignment with shoulders and knee as you press the handle forwards until arms are straight. Pause, then return to chest.

Standing Pallof Press

Stand side on to the cable column and a couple of steps back, with the handle held in at the middle of the chest. Keep a tall posture, with the feet about shoulder width apart, and maintain alignment from the ankles through the hips to the shoulders and ears. Do not allow the shoulders to shrug as you press the hands forwards, pause and return them to the middle of the chest.

Standing Pallof Press with Rotation

Set up as you would for the standing Pallof press. Press the hands forwards and, when your arms are straight, turn your shoulders away from the cable machine about seventy to eighty degrees. Keep the arms straight as you turn the shoulders and make sure you turn the hips with the movement and keep the lower back still. Rotation should come from the thoracic spine and hips, not from the lumbar spine. When turning away from the cable column, the weight shifts slightly to the outside foot and the inside leg turns with the torso, allowing the heel to lift and the toes to turn. Done correctly, this exercise will also work rotation around the femur relative to the pelvis.

Standing Pallof press, start: stand side on and a couple of feet behind a cable set at chest height. Hold the handle in at the chest and stand straight with knees slightly bent.

The stabilizing function of muscles is improved with isometric and slow eccentric contractions. The exercises at the beginning of this chapter are aimed at improving inter- and intra-muscular coordination to develop tension isometrically through the torso, to enhance stability and muscular endurance. There is then a progression to include movements that will stimulate additional stabilization and control. A variety of exercises is needed to activate different abdominal and spinal stabilization patterns, so, once a good base level of stability and endurance has been established, different exercises should be selected for each workout.

Although some focused work on this area is necessary, remember that the muscles of the core will get worked hard in different ways during the strength-training sessions too. You do not need to spend thirty minutes or more doing endless core work. Two to three sets of two to three exercises each session should be enough.

LEFT: *Standing Pallof press, continuation: keep shoulders down as you press the handle forwards and keep body straight. You should feel your abdominals automatically brace harder as you press the handle forwards. Pause in this position for a couple of seconds before returning to the start.*

OPPOSITE: *Standing Pallof press with rotation: to add a rotation, keep the arms straight after the press and turn the hips away from the cable, keeping the arms straight out in front of your chest. Rotate back and pull handle into chest and repeat.*

CHAPTER 5

DOUBLE-LEG MOVEMENTS

Some exercises attract much debate amongst coaches, therapists and athletes; squats and dead lifts are two such exercises.

Body-Weight Squats

Squats are undoubtedly a great exercise for building strength and power and for grooving motor patterns that benefit most sporting movements in some way. The squat is also a fundamental movement pattern learnt and perfected during infancy, which requires great mobility, coordination, strength and stability. Squats are not just a great strength exercise; they also can help maintain mobility at the ankles, knees and hips, and increase the strength and stability of the spine, torso, hips and legs. So why is there so much controversy over such a great exercise? The arguments against squats mostly centre on the potential stress imposed on the knees and lower back. However, it is often not the exercise that is the problem, although the application and execution might be. Correct technique is vital to make it safe and effective.

Before anyone starts loading up a bar and attempting to shift some weight they need to be able to squat properly with their body weight. Some people for various reasons may not be cut out for squatting at all and will be better off using other strengthening techniques. Tall athletes may find it hard to do back squats with good technique but may be fine with front squats, which allow for a more upright torso. Shoulder, hip and ankle mobility issues can impede squat technique and this is something that can be worked on to the benefit of much more than just improving your squats. Some people avoid squats just because they are hard work or because they don't like training their legs. Squats are hard work and that is why they are so good for building whole-body strength and a robust physique, both of which are essential for most sports. It is always worth giving squats a go and, if you are prepared to stick with it and do the work required to achieve the required mobility and control, you will reap the rewards.

Test yourself with body-weight squats first. Stand tall with feet just wider than the shoulders and hold your hands together just under your chin. Start to squat down by pushing your hips backwards and bending at the hips, knees and ankles. Keep your back straight but not vertical and your neck in line with your spine. You should be able to get deep enough so that your hip joint is slightly lower than your knee joint, but your heels remain flat on the floor, you keep a straight back and you do not fall over.

Common errors are weight shifts to one side, knees collapsing in, heels lifting off the floor, too much weight on the toes and leaning forwards, rounding the back. Causes for these errors include lack of mobility and strength in specific areas that are covered in the warm-up chapter. Errors in technique will be covered in more detail later on. For now, follow the warm-up sequence, do some SMR work, loosen up the ankles, hips and thoracic spine, then wake

Body-weight squats, side view: shoulders are over mid-thigh and foot, chest is up and back is straight. Pelvis should be tilting forwards, relative to the femur, to maintain strong lumbar spine. The depth is good with hips just below the knees and the knees just in front of the toes, with heels pressing into the floor.

Body-weight squats, front view: shoulders are level and torso sitting straight between the feet, which are just wider than the shoulders. Knees are in line with toes and feet are in neutral.

up the glutes, trunk and upper back. Another common reason for poor technique is lack of body awareness and technical knowledge of how to perform a squat.

The next step is to look at technique and a great way to develop that is with reverse pattern squats and goblet squats. Reverse patterning is a technique used by Gray Cook to help develop the squat motor pattern, while goblet squats are a big favourite with Dan John, world-renowned strength and conditioning coach, to develop good squatting technique. They are also really effective at helping to activate the muscles of the posterior chain. Holding a weight in front forces the muscles of the back to activate in order to prevent you falling forwards. They make a great specific warm-up exercise prior to squatting as well.

Reverse Pattern Squats

Reverse patterning means doing the squat from the bottom up, the way we originally learnt it as toddlers. The pattern first develops when a child is learning how to stand and that knowledge can be used to re-learn the squat. Start by sitting down on a box or chair at a comfortable height, with about ninety degrees at the knees. Eventually progress to a lower box that allows you to sit with your hips just below the level of your knees – a 12-inch box is often about right and they are commonly found in gyms. Sit up straight on the edge of the box or chair, bring the feet in towards you and place them just wider than the shoulders and pointing out very slightly. Push the knees out so they point over the middle toes and lean forwards by flexing at the hips and keeping a flat back. Push your heels down in to the floor and out at the same time, squeeze the glutes, keep the chest up and knees pushed out as you stand up straight and fully extend your hips at the top. Sit back down and repeat a few reps, this will help you

Reverse pattern squats (concentric): use a box to sit on and get yourself into the correct position for the bottom of the squat. Push your heels into the floor, squeeze glutes and keep chest up as you drive up to a standing position.

Reverse pattern squats (eccentric): to help correct technique, start standing tall in front of a box, lower yourself down a few inches, then stop, correct technique and lower down a little further. Stop again and and correct again if needed, then lower all the way to the box. Mirrors are useful at this stage to help with correcting technique.

Goblet squats, side view: this is a very similar position to the body-weight squat. The weight held at the chest allows the hips to be pushed a little further back, the back is straight with the heels down and the hips are below knees.

Goblet squats, back view: shoulders and hips are level, and knees are in line with toes, which are pointing out slightly. The heels are on the floor and feet just wider than shoulders.

to get used to being set in the right position at the bottom of a squat and wake up the dormant squat motor pattern.

When you have done a few of these try starting in an upright position with the box or chair behind you, lower half way down and pause – make sure your weight is on your heels, your back is flat and your chest s up with your shoulders over the middle of your feet – then lower the rest of the way to the box or chair. Relax, then set yourself in the bottom position and stand back up. This is another excellent way to quickly improve strength, develop awareness and correct technique.

Goblet Squats

Stand tall with feet about shoulder width apart and pointing out slightly, holding a dumbbell vertically by one end or a kettlebell by the horns close to the chest and under the chin with elbows held in against the ribs. Now start the descent by pushing the hips backwards then lowering down, bending at the hips, knees and ankles as if sitting down to a chair. Most people seem to be under-active in the glutes, which makes them quad-dominant when they squat and causes them to put too much weight on the toes. Make sure you put weight through the heels and push the knees out so that they travel in line with the middle toes. At the bottom of the squat the hips should be slightly lower than the knees. Keep the chest up to maintain a flat back and look straight ahead. A good depth can be achieved by touching the elbows to the thighs at the bottom. Hold the bottom position for two to three seconds – this isometric contraction will help to groove a correct posture and quickly improve strength at the weakest part of the squat movement. To stand back up, push your heels in to the floor, squeeze your glutes and keep your knees pushed out in line with the toes. Lift your chest as you drive up

fast, squeezing the glutes at the top to make sure you finish the movement by standing up straight.

Work on developing your body-weight squats with reverse patterning and goblet squats until you can squat with perfect form and control. Only then should you get under a bar and start squatting with heavy weights.

Back Squats with a Bar

It is important to understand the proper technique for back squats using an Olympic bar. Make sure the bar is racked just below the height of the shoulders so you can safely un-rack and rack it without having to rise up on to your toes. This should be common-sense safety. Olympic bars have a ring of smooth steel half way along the knurling on each side, which should be used to make sure you have an even grip. Most people should have their hands just inside these rings for the right grip width, but it does depend on how big you are. The hands should be slightly wider than the shoulders, not out wide to the ends of the bar. The narrow grip allows you to pull your elbows and shoulder blades in to activate the lats and upper back. Hold with an overhand or pronated grip and move under the bar with the feet directly beneat. The hips and knees should be slightly flexed and the bar placed across the top of the shoulder blades. Do not rest the bar on your neck. It should be resting on the ridge created by your depressed scapulars and upper trapezius muscles. Lift your chest and pull the bar on to your upper traps to keep it in place. This will also activate the lats that will help to stabilize the spine.

Lift the bar off the rack and carefully take a couple of steps back. Stand straight with the feet slightly wider than the shoulders, to allow for optimal contribution from all the muscles in

Back squat, bar position: the hands hold the bar slightly wider than shoulders. The bar is placed on top of the shoulder blades, with the shoulders pulled down.

Back squat, start position: move back from the squat stands and stand up straight with feet just wider than shoulders and pointing out slightly. Squeeze shoulder blades together and pull bar down to activate the lats. Brace abdominals, shift weight to heels and push hips back to start the descent.

the legs and hips, and more depth in the squat. Although having the feet just wider than the shoulders is optimal for most people, the width of the stance can be adjusted slightly to allow for differences in hip structure between individuals. Find the width that allows you to achieve the correct depth while at the same time maintaining a flat back. The feet can point out slightly – between about five and ten degrees.

Start the descent by pushing the hips back and flexing the hips and knees. Do not tilt the pelvis forwards. Keep the back straight and push the hips back. Pull the bar down on to your upper traps and keep your chest up. The neck should stay in line with the spine. Do not look up or down but pull your chin in slightly to 'pack' your neck. This is the term used by physical therapist and strength and conditioning coach Charlie Weingroff to describe the best neck position to increase spinal stability and help you lift more weight. Keep your knees pushed out in line with your middle toes and keep your weight back on your heels. As you descend further this is when you start to tilt the pelvis forwards to maintain a straight back as you flex more at the hips. The bar should travel down in line with the mid-foot. As you reach the bottom position the hips are back and the knees may be over the toes or just in front of them, depending on the length of your legs, torso and other anatomical factors. For most people in the bottom position the bar will be over about mid-thigh and mid-foot and the hips should be just below the knees. Kinetic energy is produced during the descent through stored elastic energy in the lengthening muscles and fascia and at the bottom point you will have to stop the descent in order to start coming back up. This may only be for a split second – which makes it an explosive isometric contraction – and is part of the stretch shortening cycle. Coupled with the concentric contraction, this produces the power to drive you back up.

From the bottom position you keep everything tight to start the ascent. Keep the neck packed in line with the spine, the shoulder blades pulled together and lats tight. Your abdominals should be braced just enough to maintain stability and your back needs to be flat and tight. Push your heels into the floor and out at the same time, squeeze your glutes hard and drive yourself up using the power from the hips. Make sure you stand up straight at the top and do not keep your hips flexed. Squeeze the glutes and get the hips under the bar. The bar should remain over the mid-foot the whole time.

A Note on Abdominal Bracing

Bracing the abs is an important part of spine stabilization and force transference but should not be overdone. When lifting heavy weights strong abdominal bracing is needed, the heavier the load the stronger the brace. During light work you should brace only as much as is needed to perform safely and efficiently, and to achieve the movement with proper technique and control. Over-bracing will waste energy and put the spine under unnecessary compressive load. When using heavy weights the Valsalva manoeuvre should be employed. Before the descent take a deep breath, let a little out, then hold your breath and brace your abs. Hold your breath during the descent, then slowly let some out through pursed lips during the ascent, while maintaining a strong brace.

Squats are great for developing strength and power in the torso, hips and legs and can be manipulated with tempo, volume and weight to elicit different adaptations depending on training goals. Aside from the obvious strength adaptations, most sporting actions also benefit from the activation patterns and force generation profiles of the squat.

Back squat, bottom position: the hips are just below the knees and the bar is still in place on top of the shoulder blades and over the mid-foot. The back stays straight and the pelvis tilts forwards to prevent the lumbar spine rounding.

Back squat, finish position: push the heels down and out and lift your chest as you drive back up to the start position and finish with the hips under the bar.

Common Errors and Correction

Sometimes, movement errors can occur when you start squatting, but most can be corrected with the right interventions. The majority are due to a combination of factors such as past injuries or frequently held postures, such as sitting down for ten hours a day, which can result in muscle imbalances and postural and movement dysfunctions. Mobility and activation methods (covered in the training preparation phase of this book) should be the main focus of attention until you are moving better and can squat deep and with perfect form with body weight only. You need to be aware of what is going wrong before you can consciously effect a positive change. Look out for the various errors (see below) in your own squats and, if they are present, try using the corrective techniques.

Kinaesthetic awareness is the ability to know where your body is in relation to its surroundings and to itself – how far apart your feet are, the position of your pelvis relative to your femur and the shape of your spine, for example. Think of it as a sixth sense and try to develop it as much as you can. The walls of most gyms are covered in mirrors and, although these can be of help to give you some initial feedback, using them all the time will hinder development of your kinaesthetic awareness. Use the mirrors in the beginning if they help you get the movement right, then try to develop a feel for the movement without them. A good technique used by the Russian weightlifters is to do a few reps with your eyes shut. This heightens awareness and helps to improve coordination and neural excitement for the rest of the workout. Remember to be aware of your body and think about the alignment of joints, weight distribution and muscle tension. Feel what is going on when you are trying to develop technique.

The use of bar pads and lifting belts is often connected with body awareness. Bar pads should be avoided, however, as they make it easy to place the bar in the wrong place. It usually ends up high on the shoulders, loading up the cervical spine, which is potentially very dangerous. You should be able to feel the bar resting on your upper back and it is supposed to be uncomfortable when you first put a heavy weight on there. That is your body telling you to be careful. After a couple of sets you will find the discomfort eases, as you become accustomed to that particular weight. Without a pad it is easier to get and feel the bar in the right place and then you are set up to get the squat right.

Lifting belts should be avoided as much as possible and only used for serious all-out efforts. Such efforts should not even be attempted by any but the most advanced lifters.

Your shoes or footwear should have hard flat soles. Running shoes have soft cushioned soles for absorbing forces; they are for running, not for weight training. You do not want to lose force through your shoes when you are trying to get stronger; instead, you want to transfer it from the floor through your body to the bar. The other problem with soft shoes is that they create an unstable surface between you and the floor. If the surface is constantly shifting beneath your feet the nervous system cannot develop and groove the activation pattern needed for optimum force development. You need to train on a hard stable surface to get strong especially when the legs are involved.

Squat Depth

One very common error is not going deep enough. Many people load up the bar with more weight than they can actually squat, bend their knees a little five times, then put the bar back. Being able to move a big weight a few inches is not strong. Strong is being able to move a weight through a full range of movement with good technique and that means getting deep enough so that your hip joints are just below the level of your knees. The right depth is needed to get a stretch on the glutes and use the resulting SSC to help drive you up. The glutes are the biggest muscles in the body and can contribute a lot of power to a lot of movements, so you must make sure you get deep enough to strengthen them. If you cannot achieve the correct depth, look at the mobility of your ankles, hips and thoracic spine, and use goblet squats (see page 93) to help develop your technique. You may make the correction simply by reducing the weight.

Too Much Weight on the Toes

Putting too much weight through the ball of the foot usually results in the bar being in front of the mid-foot and the knees going too far in front of the toes. Quite often the heels will lift off the floor as well, putting you off balance and placing too much load on the knees. Weight on the toes makes the movement too quad-dominant. Instead, the weight needs to be shifted backwards to the heels, especially as you get deeper. Lack of awareness is a factor in most technique errors and simply pushing the hips back and shifting some weight to the heels is enough to get in the right position. Once that position has been found, it can be grooved.

Over-activation in the quads and/or hamstrings, or lack of activation in the glutes or even the whole posterior chain can all be part of the problem. Often, all these factors are involved. Do the SMR exercises to reduce tension in the hip flexors, quads, glutes and biceps femoris, then go through some mobility drills and activation work from the training preparation/warm-up section (see pages 16–57), and develop technique with reverse patterning or goblet squats.

Back squat error – weight too far forward: this is an extreme forward weight shift, with the heels coming up off the floor. The error is often more subtle than this but the result is the same: the work is being done by the quads and the weight is going through the knees and the toes.

Lateral Weight Shift

A lateral weight shift is often to the dominant side or as a result of an injury or learned pattern from daily activities or held postures. The shift can occur on the way down or on the way back up, and sometimes in both directions. Look for tender spots in both legs and hips with the foam roller and mobilize (see pages 18–21). Increase neural drive to the weaker leg with single-leg exercises. Afterwards, when you squat, be aware of what is happening and try to adjust your weight distribution. A good way to do this is to use a light weight and descend slowly, stopping at two or three points for a couple of seconds along the way to adjust your position.

Knees Collapsing In

You may find that your knees move in as you descend or as you push back up from the bottom of the squat. This can occur with both knees simultaneously or just one. Again, it is usually a result of muscle imbalance and lack of awareness and technique. If the muscles on the outside of the hips, thigh and lower leg are suffering from too much tension, this can cause the knee to move in when you squat. Over-active adductors can also cause the same problem especially when the glutes are under-active. SMR is required for all these areas as is thorough activation for glutes, max and medius.

When you start to squat, make sure you have your weight on your heels and push your knees out, in line with your toes, as you descend. On the way up, push your heels down and out into the floor at the same time and think about squeezing your glutes and keeping your knees in line with your toes.

Mini bands are excellent for forcing activation of the glutes during a squat – these muscles control femoral rotation and prevent the knees from collapsing in. Place the band around the legs just below the knees, feet just

Back squat error – lateral weight shift: here, the weight has shifted to the right on the way down. Watch the squat carefully because the error can be quite subtle – it can move from one side to the other, or be fine on the way down and shift on the way up.

Back squat error – knees collapsing in: here, the right knee is moving in during the descent (valgus collapse), which increases the risk of knee injury. You may see both knees collapsing in.

a bit more than shoulder width apart, then do a body-weight squat (see page 90). Make sure you keep the knees pushed out against the band so that they remain in line with your toes.

Rounding the Back

The back muscles should be tight when squatting and the spine held still, with some thoracic extension. During the descent the hips should flex and the pelvis should tilt anteriorly to help prevent the hips tucking under and causing the lumbar spine to flex. Flexion at the lumbar or thoracic regions will produce excessive compressive and shear loading on the spine and can result in injury and a loss of force or power production through poor mechanics. Tightness in the glutes, biceps fermoris and adductors can hinder pelvic mobility, so use SMR and mobility drills (see the warm-

up section) to loosen these areas. Lack of thoracic extension is another factor that may need improving. Again, do some SMR for the upper back, some mobility work for the thoracic spine and activation for thoracic extension (see the warm-up/preparation phase, pages 28–31 for some examples).

Activation of the back muscles and posterior chain in general is required for proper technique and holding a weight in front, as in goblet squats, is a good way to achieve this, to prevent you falling forwards. Another technique is wall squats. Stand facing a wall, a few inches away, with hands clasped under your chin, keep looking straight ahead and do a squat. If this is easy, stand a bit closer to the wall and try again. If you fail to get enough thoracic extension your head will hit the wall or you will fall backwards. The idea is to avoid both.

Back squat error – rounding the back: the rounded back position is very dangerous for the spine and needs to be fixed before resuming back squats. The back can appear straight until you near the bottom of the squat, when the lumbar spine rounds out. Sometimes the lumbar spine is fine but the thoracic spine rounds. Watch out for these errors and work on correcting them.

Front Squats with a Bar

Front squats are a great variation for developing strength and power in the legs and hips. They involve placing the bar across the front of the shoulders instead of across the upper back. Front squats place less load on the lumbar spine, with a bit more emphasis on the quads. They are also good preparation for the Olympic lifts and their derivatives.

Start by clasping the bar with a grip slightly wider than shoulder width. Move both feet under the bar with knees slightly bent, back straight and the bar resting on the front deltoids. Lift the elbows high so that the upper arm is parallel to the floor and the elbows point forwards. Brace your abs slightly, lift the bar off the rack and move back a couple of steps. Stand tall with feet just wider than shoulder width – this can be varied slightly to allow for individual differences, but the bar should still be held in the hands, resting on the front deltoids and just lightly touching the front of the neck.

Start the descent as you would for any other squat by pushing the hips back without tilting the pelvis and flexing at the ankles knees and hips. Keep your chest up, elbows high and neck packed as you descend. The front squat bottom position has a slightly more upright torso than the back squat. It must be deep enough to get the hips just below the knees and the back must be flat with elbows high and chest up. Start the ascent by pushing the heels down and out into the floor, squeezing the glutes and driving up without dropping the elbows or chest and keeping the back straight.

Front squat, bar position: the hands are just wider than the shoulders, with the elbows high and the bar resting across the front of the shoulders.

Front squat: at the bottom of the front squat the elbows should still be held high, with the chest up, back straight, weight over the mid-foot and hips just below knees.

Front squat alternative grip: this grip will allow you to front squat if you lack the mobility to use the normal grip. Use it if you need to, but try to develop the mobility to use the proper grip.

The common errors and their corrections are similar to those of the back squat (see pages 98–99), with the exception of the shoulders. Some people find it difficult to get the elbows up into the right position. It requires good mobility in the thoracic spine, shoulders and wrist, and practising front squats is one way to gradually improve this mobility needed. If you intend to start doing some form of cleans it is essential to develop the ability to perform front squats with this grip. If you want to front squat but the proper grip is too uncomfortable, use the alternate grip: cross over your forearms and hold the bar with a supinated grip, with the hands close together. Move under the bar and place it across the front deltoids. Now you should be holding the bar with elbows high and pointing forwards, with the bar just lightly touching the front of your neck and resting on your front deltoids.

Overhead Squats

Overhead squats build a different kind of strength using much lighter loads, unless you are very accomplished at the Olympic lifts and are capable of snatching a big weight. Holding the weight over your head raises your centre of gravity, challenging whole-body balance over the full range of the movement. Although the load may be comparatively light for the hips and legs, there is a much greater need for mobility, stability and strength in the arms and shoulders.

Overhead squat, start position: stand straight with feet just wider than shoulders, holding the bar overhead with arms straight and elbows locked. Keep the bar over the crown of the head.

Overhead squat, bottom position: lower the hips just below the level of the knees, keeping the back straight and the knees in line with the toes. Hold the bar above the crown of the head with arms straight and neck in line with the spine.

Start standing tall with the bar held overhead with a wide grip, arms straight and elbows locked, feet just wider than shoulders. The arms should be level with the ears and the bar over the crown of the head. Start the descent in the same way as for the back squat by pushing the hips back and flexing from hips, knees and ankles as you start to lower down. Keep the knees in line with the middle toes and get deep enough for the hips to break parallel, just below the level of the knees. In this deep position the back is kept tight and flat and the hips are flexed so that the torso leans forwards enough for the shoulders to be over the mid-foot, directly under the bar. Keep the scapulars depressed throughout, do not allow the humerus to rotate medially and drive the humeral head into the anterior joint capsule. Keep the neck in line with the spine. Start the ascent by keeping the abdominals braced and the back muscles tight. Push the heels down and out into the floor and drive up to a full standing position with the hips under the shoulders.

Dead Lifts

The dead lift is another great exercise that is often misunderstood and avoided due to the belief that it will damage the spine. This is misguided – once again, it is inappropriate application or poor execution that can cause problems. The dead lift will strengthen the legs, hips, back and torso, as well as the shoulders and arms. It really is a whole-body exercise. Dead lifts and squats are great exercises for developing lower-body strength and power, with the biomechanical differences making the dead lift a hip-dominant exercise and the squat a quad-dominant exercise. This is important to remember when you are devising a training plan. All squat and dead-lift variations will help develop a strong back as long as the technique is correct and you increase the weight gradually to allow for adaptation.

Olympic Bar Dead Lift

Stand with your toes under the bar and feet about shoulder width apart. Flex the knees and hips and reach down to grasp the bar outside the width of the feet with a pronated (overhand) grip. In the start position the heels are flat on the floor, the knees in line with the toes and the arms straight. The hips should be about half way between the level of the knees and the shoulders and the back held flat with the neck in line with the spine. A correct position at the start of the dead lift is vital to safe and effective performance and a

Olympic bar dead lift (isometric set position): place the toes under the bar then flex hips and knees to grasp bar outside of the knees. Shift weight to heels and move hips back so that the knees are just behind the bar and the hips are half way between shoulders and knees. Lift chest and pull shoulder blades together as you pull on the bar and push heels into the floor without lifting the weight. Hold this isometric contraction for three to five seconds.

good way to groove a set position is to use an isometric contraction.

Put more weight on the bar than you can lift and get into the start position. Push the hips back a little so that the knees are just behind the bar and put your weight through the heels. Push the chest out and pull the shoulders back. Keep the arms straight and pre-load the bar by pulling on it and taking up any slack. Brace the abdominals, push the heels down and out into the floor, push the chest out and pull hard on the bar for about five seconds without moving. Relax and stand back up, leaving the bar on the floor. Rest for around two minutes and repeat.

To perform the whole lift get into the start position and pre-load the bar as described above, then simultaneously pull on the bar and push the floor down and out through the heels and stand up, keeping the abdominals braced and the back straight. Finish the lift by squeezing the glutes at the top and pushing the hips forwards and pulling the shoulders back until you are standing straight but not leaning back. To return the bar, keep the chest up and the back straight, push the hips back and hinge at the hips to lower the bar to the knees, then flex the knees to lower the bar to the floor. Keep the abdominals braced all the way down until you have released the bar and stood back up.

When the weight starts to get too heavy to lift with a pronated grip you can change to an alternate grip, which will enable you to lift a lot more weight without the bar slipping out of your hands. Hold the bar with a pronated or overhand grip with one hand and a supernated or underhand grip with the other.

Tall athletes may need to raise the barbell off the ground on to some low blocks or boxes, to allow for better technique. The distance of the bar from the floor is determined by the diameter of the plates and the best weightlifters and power lifters tend to have the right body shape and proportions conducive to lifting heavy weights from this position. If on the other hand you are quite tall with long limbs, you might have trouble getting into the right

Olympic bar dead lift, start: get into the set position then push heels down and out, lift chest, pull shoulder blades together, pre-load the bar and brace abdominals.

Olympic bar dead lift, continuation: pull the bar off the floor while simultaneously pushing heels down and driving hips forwards.

Olympic bar dead lift, finish: stand up straight at the finish with shoulders back, hips forward and glutes squeezed. Do not lean back, but lift the chest and stand up straight.

Alternative grip for dead lift: when the weight gets too heavy to hold with a pronated grip, turn one hand round to a supinated grip. This will allow you to lift more weight.

position to lift safely. Do not risk your back if you cannot get into the correct position. Instead, raise the bar off the floor and it will still be a great strength-building exercise. As a rough guide the bar should be at least half way up your shins. If you are lucky enough to have access to a set of technique boxes then the top, smallest, box usually provides enough height if it is needed.

Sumo Dead Lift

The Sumo dead lift involves a wider stance and stimulates greater activation from the adductors to perform the lift. It still develops great strength in the posterior chain, shoulders and arms and provides good variation for your training.

Stand with your toes under the bar and feet about twice shoulder width apart, point the toes out slightly and keep the knees in line with them as you push the hips back and reach down to grasp the bar with a narrow grip inside the knees. The starting position will be a little more upright in the torso than for the conventional dead lift, but the action is very similar. From here the lift is the same as above: weight through heels, abdominals braced, chest up and neck in line with spine. Pre-load the bar by pulling up and extending the thoracic spine while squeezing the glutes and pushing the heels into the floor, then pull the bar off the floor and push the hips forwards until standing straight.

Sumo dead lift, start: a great exercise to stretch the adductors under load, start with the feet wide, about twice shoulder width and hold the bar inside of the knees about shoulder width.

Sumo dead lift, finish: pre-load the bar as you would for the normal dead lift, then press your heels into the floor and pull the bar up at the same time. Keep chest up and shoulders back and stand up straight with hips forward at the finish.

Stiff-Leg Dead Lift

If you play a sport that involves any running about, you ought to be doing this exercise. Hamstring injuries are more common than they should be in running sports and the main reasons are lack of understanding, preparation and bad training techniques. The hamstring has to contract eccentrically to slow down and control the lower leg as it swings forwards during running and kicking. If the hamstring is not used to a rapid lengthening, the myotatic reflex can activate and trigger a contraction that conflicts with the need to lengthen. Stiff-leg dead lifts train the nervous system to improve inter- and intra-muscular coordination as well as eccen-

tric strength, which will reduce the risk of hamstring injuries.

Unlike the other two versions of the dead lift, the stiff-leg dead lift starts in the standing position with knees slightly bent. It is so called because, from here on, the knees remain stiff and the movement comes from the hips. The emphasis with this exercise is on the lower back, glutes and hamstrings. Because the origin of the hamstrings is on the pelvis (ischial tuberosity), keeping the knees stiff and flexing from the hips means that the hamstrings and glutes are lengthened under load while an isometric contraction increases back strength and stability. Since this lift starts from a standing position there is a build-up of kinetic energy from the lengthening glutes and hamstrings, which helps with returning to the starting position, together with the concentric contraction of the glutes and hamstrings during hip extension.

To start, dead lift the weight off the floor and stand tall with the feet hip to shoulder width apart, and hands holding the bar at about shoulder width. The grip can be overhand or alternate, depending on how strong your grip is. Bend the knees slightly, shift your weight to your heels and lift your chest while keeping your neck in line with your spine. Start pushing the hips back and flexing from the hips. Keep your shoulders back and chest up to maintain a tight and straight back. Stop when you feel a good stretch in the hamstrings then return to an upright position and squeeze the glutes to get a full hip extension. Let the stretch in the hamstrings guide the range of movement and do not lower your chest in an attempt to get the bar closer to the floor.

Stiff-leg dead lift, start: hold the bar with a shoulder-width grip and stand up straight with feet about hip width apart, chest up and shoulders down. Bend the knees slightly, shift weight to your heels and push the hips back to start the movement.

Stiff-leg dead lift, finish: maintain the small knee bend as you flex from the hips and keep your chest up and your back straight. Squeeze glutes and drive the hips forwards to return to the start.

Getting the hip hinge movement right can be a bit tricky so it might be a good idea to work on it without a weight first. Try standing with your back to a wall, about a foot away, with your arms held across your chest. Shift your weight to your heels and push your hips back until you touch the wall with your glutes. Keep your neck in line with your spine, pull your shoulders back and push your chest out to tighten your back and keep your spine still as you hinge from the hips. Practise this movement first if you find it difficult to maintain the right back position when you hinge forwards. Standing side on to a mirror can give good initial feedback to help with getting the hinge right.

Developing Strength in the Posterior Chain

These next two exercises are great for developing strength in the posterior chain espe-

cially the glutes. The reason we have glutes is to enable us to stand upright and move around and strong glutes are vital for forward propulsion. If you play a sport that involves running, you ought to do some serious training for this area.

Pull-Through

Set a cable to the bottom setting and attach the rope or a V-shaped handle. Stand a couple of feet away with your back to the cable column holding the rope attachment between your legs. Stand up straight and walk forwards a couple more feet to lift the weight stack up about half way. Bend your knees slightly, keep your arms straight and perform the hip hinge. Transfer your weight to your heels and push your hips back as you bend forwards from the hips. Keep your chest up, shoulders down and maintain a neutral spine. Keep your arms straight and let your hands move back between your legs. Stop when you feel a stretch in the

Pull-through, start: use a rope attachment if you have one and stand astride the cable holding the ends of the rope in front with straight arms and hips fully extended. Move a couple of feet forwards from the cable column.

Pull-through, finish: bend knees a little and keep arms straight as you hinge forwards from the hips and allow your hands to move back between your legs. Stop when you feel a nice stretch in your hamstrings then squeeze your glutes, drive your hips forwards and stand up straight.

hamstrings, then squeeze your glutes hard and drive your hips forwards, pulling the cable through with your hands at the same time. You should finish standing tall with your hips fully extended and your arms straight, holding the cable just in front of your hips.

Hip Thrusts

Hip thrusts are similar to the bridge lifts in the warm-up section but with the use of a bench, an Olympic bar and some weight. Start with just the bar first to get a feel for it, then gradually add some weight. To begin, sit in front of a bench with your upper back resting against the bench and your knees bent, feet on the floor and arms across your chest. From this start position, push your hips up off the floor until they are slightly higher than your shoulders and knees. Your lower legs should be perpendicular to the floor and your shoulders/upper back supported on the bench. This is the finish position. To add weight, place a bar across the hips and lift up, squeezing your glutes. As you get stronger and start using big plates you should be able to fit under the bar and drive up from the start position.

Hip thrusts, start: keep the knees in line with the hips and ankles as you push your heels into the floor squeeze the glutes and drive the hips up. Keep the back straight and neck in line with the spine throughout.

Hip thrusts, finish: stop with the hips in line or just above the level of the knees and shoulders. Make sure the extension comes from the hips and not the lumbar spine.

CHAPTER 6

SINGLE-LEG MOVEMENTS

Single-leg exercises provide a multi-dimensional challenge. They require a lot of stability through the torso, hips, knees and ankles and this makes them an essential part of any serious training regime. Single-leg strength is also a vital ingredient in performance enhancement as most sports involve single-leg actions requiring eccentric, concentric and isometric strength in all planes of movement.

Split Squats

Basic Technique

Split squats are a good exercise to start developing single-leg strength. Although both feet are on the floor and both legs are contributing to the movement, the actions of the two legs are very different. The front leg flexes at the knee and hip while the rear leg flexes at the knee and extends at the hip. Frontal plane stability is challenged and opposing hip extension flexion, which is important to locomotion, is promoted and placed under load. Place the bar in the same position as for the back squats and un-rack it in the same way. Stand tall, with the bar resting across the top of the shoulder blades, and pull down on the bar, squeezing the shoulder blades together. Keep the chest up as you take a step about twice shoulder width back with your left leg. This is the start position. Now flex the knees and lower down to the floor, stopping just short of touching the floor or touching it very lightly with your left knee. At the bottom the knees should be at ninety degrees

and the left knee should be aligned with the hip and shoulder. Keep the torso straight as you press the right heel and ball of the left foot into the floor and squeeze the glutes as you stand back up to the start position.

This exercise can also be performed holding a dumbbell in each hand, which makes it a little easier due to a lower centre of gravity.

Split squats: place the bar across the top of the shoulder blades as for the back squat and stand with feet split about twice shoulder width.

Split squats: keep the torso straight as you descend. If the stance is right you should have knees bent to ninety degrees at the bottom. Push the front heel into the floor to stand back up with help from the back foot.

Errors and Correction

There are two major errors to look for, which often go together: shifting too much weight on to the toes of the front foot and flexing at the hips, which is sometimes the result of pushing the hips backwards. Failure to keep your torso and rear thigh perpendicular to the floor during the descent and ascent can be due to a tightness in the hip flexors, lack of glute and core activation, and/or lack of stability. All of these things can be part of the problem and should be addressed with some work on glute and core activation and hip mobility, covered in the preparation phase. Quite often the problem is just a lack of technique

with too much reliance on the front leg to stand back up. Make sure you push up with the rear leg at the same time as pushing the heel of the front leg into the floor. This will also correct the other common error of shifting weight on to the front toes.

Rear Foot Elevated Split Squats (RFESS)

This is a great variation of the split squat that shifts more of the workload to the front-leg quads and glute and provides eccentric loading for the quads and hip flexors of the rear leg. This exercise can also be performed with a bar across the upper back or holding dumbbells in the hands. Start by standing straight

RFESS (rear foot elevated split squats): when the foot is elevated the distance between the feet should be about twice shoulder width, with most of the weight on the front foot. Keep the chest up and shoulders down.

113

RFESS (rear foot elevated split squats): lower the hips straight down and flex both knees. Most of the weight and work is on the front foot. Push the heel of the front foot down to stand back up.

Step-ups, start: stand tall with one foot on a box that is high enough to achieve an angle at the knee of just under ninety degrees.

about a metre in front of a bench or box, place the ball of the left foot on the box behind and keep the chest up and shoulders down. Keep the torso straight as you start the descent and maintain this throughout. In the bottom position, the right (front) knee should be just over and in line with the middle toes, with the heel on the floor and the left (back) knee just off the floor behind the mid-line of the torso. Start the ascent by pushing the front foot, particularly the heel, into the floor, drive yourself back up to the start position and finish standing tall with the hips under the shoulders.

Step-Ups

Basic Technique

Step-ups can also be performed with a barbell across the upper back or holding dumbbells at the sides. If using dumbbells do not allow the shoulders to drop into a slouched position; keep the torso straight and chest up. If using a barbell, make sure it is resting across the top of the shoulder blades, use a narrow grip and squeeze the shoulder blades together as for the squat set-up.

Stand up straight in front of a step-up box about knee height and place the right foot flat on the step. The right knee and hip should form an angle of about ninety degrees, or the hip should be just lower than the knee. Lean forwards slightly by flexing at the hips so that the shoulders are over the mid-foot, keep the chest up and the back straight. Push the right foot into the box, squeeze the glutes and drive up to a standing position, placing your left foot next to your right foot on the box. Step down with the left leg, leaving the right foot on the box, then repeat.

There are a couple of different ways to perform step-ups. Depending on your ability to balance and control the weight, you can

Step-ups, continuation: push the heel down on the box and, with as little help as possible from the rear foot, extend the front leg and stand up on to the box. You can flex forwards slightly from the hips, especially when the weight gets heavy but make sure the back stays straight.

hold the top position on one leg. Step up and hold the left leg straight just behind or flex the left hip and knee to ninety degrees and balance for a second or two before stepping back down.

Lateral Step-Ups

Stand side on to a step-up box about the height of your knee with dumbbells in the hands or a bar across the shoulders. Start-

ing with dumbbells makes it slightly easier to maintain your balance. Place the inside foot on top of the box, keep your body straight as you press your foot, especially the heel, in to the box and stand up. Straighten the leg and fully extend the hips at the top, squeezing your glutes. Keep your chest up and shoulders down. Then transfer your weight to your heel and keep it down on the step as you lower your outside foot back down to the floor, and repeat.

Lateral step-ups, start: stand side on to the box, a couple of feet away, and place the nearest foot on to it, in line with the foot on the floor.

Lateral step-ups, continuation: keep the heel pushed down as you stand up on to the box, balance on one leg for a second then return to the start.

Step-ups/lateral step-ups, alternative finish: lift the knee of the free leg high and straighten out the standing leg without tilting the hips or torso.

Lunges

Although forward and reverse lunges look very similar they are very different in their recruitment patterns. The reverse lunge is a hip-dominant exercise that strengthens the pattern for forward propulsion during the concentric phase, whereas forward lunges help strengthen deceleration patterns. Both versions involve being on one leg for part of the movement, requiring balance and stability and greater activation from the glutes.

Reverse Lunge Technique

Start standing up straight with feet hip width apart and a dumbbell in each hand or a barbell across the top of the shoulder blades, as for the squat. Take a step back about twice shoulder width and lower down, bending the knees until the rear knee is just touching the floor and both are bent to ninety degrees. Keep the chest up and torso straight. The rear knee

Reverse lunge/forward lunge/walking lunge, start position: the starting position is the same for reverse, forward and walking lunges. Stand up straight with feet hip width apart and arms by the sides holding dumbbells in the hands.

Reverse lunge: take a big step back and lower to the floor, keeping torso straight and chest up. The knees should be at ninety degrees at the bottom. Then return to the start, pushing the front heel into the floor and keeping the knee in line with the hip and ankle.

should be kept in line with the hip and shoulder at the bottom position. Push the front heel into the floor and squeeze the glutes to drive you back up to the starting position.

Errors and Correction

To avoid taking too big or too small a step back try a couple of practice steps without weight to gauge your correct distance. At the bottom of the movement the knees should be at ninety degrees and the torso straight.

As for the split squat some people make the mistake of leaning too far forwards, either on the way down or on the way up. Mobilize the hip flexors and work on firing up the glutes and torso to improve stability. Keep the chest up and look straight ahead during the movement and squeeze the glutes; this should also help to keep your torso straight. Work on developing the technique using just body weight to begin with.

The front knee can collapse in either during the descent (eccentric phase) or the ascent (concentric phase). Tight hip flexors, ITB or adductors can contribute to this, as can a lack of control from the glute max and med. If the TFL and ITB are tight they can cause valgus collapse (the knee collapsing inwards), while tightness at the front of the hip will inhibit the glutes. Use SMR to ease some of the tension in the TFL/hip flexors, adductors and ITB, then mobilize the hips before activating the glute max and med. Making sure the glutes are working properly will help to control internal rotation of the femur and help prevent valgus collapse (the knee collapsing inwards). Work on technique with just body weight for resistance at first. As you push the front heel into the floor, squeeze the glutes and think about pushing the knee out to keep it in line with the hip and ankle.

Forward Lunge Technique

The start is the same as for the reverse lunge, standing tall with dumbbells in the hands or the barbell across the top of the shoulder blades. Keep the shoulders down and the chest up and the neck in line with the spine. Take a step forwards about twice shoulder width in length and lower the back knee to the floor. You should have ninety degrees at the knees, with the rear knee in line with the hip and shoulder and the front knee in line with the hip and ankle. Keep the chest up and press the front heel into the floor to push yourself back up to the start position.

The errors and corrections are very similar to the ones for the reverse lunge. One error more common with the forward lunge is due to forward momentum when the front foot is planted on the ground. The front knee can travel too far in front of the toes and the heel comes up off the floor. Make sure the step forwards is the right length by lowering the back knee to the floor and setting the

Forward lunge: take a big forward step and lower to the floor, keeping chest up and shoulders aligned with the down knee and hip. To return to the start, push off the front foot keeping the heel down and the knee in line with the hip and ankle.

knees to ninety degrees with the torso and the rear thigh perpendicular to the floor. Place a marker on the floor to maintain step length, concentrate on achieving ninety degrees at the knees and press the front heel into the floor.

Walking Lunges

Walking lunges involve deceleration, acceleration and balance and stability during the step-through phase, all of which makes for a great exercise. There must be adequate mobility and stability through the ankles, knees, hips and torso if you are to perform this exercise correctly, so make sure you have worked on these factors and perfected the other versions first.

Start standing tall with dumbbells in your hands by your sides. Take a step forwards that is big enough to achieve ninety degrees at the knees, as you would for the forward lunge.

Lower down until the rear knee is just off the floor, then stop and push the front heel into the floor to drive you up to a standing position. As you near the standing position, start to bring your rear leg forwards and step right through to a forward lunge. Repeat the motion for the desired number of steps. Try not to break it down into separate parts of lunge, split squat and stand, but perform it as a fluid movement, stepping forwards, down, up and through. Do not allow the front knee to collapse in; see the advice on knee alignment when doing reverse lunges (see page 116).

Lateral Lunges

Stand tall with the chest up and shoulders down and take a step to the side about twice shoulder width. As you step to the side, flex from the hips slightly, bend the knee of the leg

Lateral lunge: start standing straight, holding a dumbbell in close to your chest. Take a big step to one side about twice shoulder width. Bend the stepping leg and lower the hips until they are level with the knee, then push back to the start. Keep the back straight but flex from the hips as you lower them down.

that moves to the side and keep the stationary leg straight. Land with the toes pointing out slightly and keep the heel on the floor as you bend the knee to about ninety degrees, keeping it in line with the toes. Keep the back flat with the chest up and shoulders over the bent knee, then push the heel down and drive yourself back up to a standing position, and repeat.

To make it harder try holding a dumbbell at your chest as you would for a goblet squat or use a barbell across the shoulders.

Single-Leg Stiff-Leg Dead Lift

This is a great exercise for working the posterior chain and loading the hamstring and glutes while resisting rotation through the hips and spine. There are a couple of different ways to perform it. The first version uses a single dumbbell held in the hand opposite to the standing leg. Keep your chest up and shoulders down, stand on your left leg with your right foot just off the floor and knee slightly bent and hold the dumbbell in your right hand. Bend the left knee slightly and start to flex forwards from the hips, putting the weight through the left heel and pushing the hips back. Keep the chest up, extend the thoracic spine to maintain a tight back and straighten the right leg out behind. Keep the right hip square to the floor. Stop the forward flexion when you feel a good stretch in the left hamstring, then return to the starting position. Put your right foot down for a momentary rest between repetitions if you need to. If you can, try to balance on your left leg through the whole set of repetitions – you will feel a lot more work going on through the left leg and hip.

Another way to perform this exercise is to hold a barbell in the hands. This allows you to use larger weights as you get stronger. The starting position is the same, standing up tall

Single-leg stiff-leg dead lift, start: stand straight on one leg, holding a dumbbell in the hand opposite to that leg.

119

Single-leg stiff-leg dead lift, continuation: keep a small bend in the standing leg and flex from the hips while keeping the spine and pelvis neutral. Extend the free leg at the same time and keep the hips square.

with the shoulders down and chest up, the neck in line with spine and a small bend in the knee of the standing leg. Hold the barbell in front of you at mid-thigh with the arms straight, using an overhand grip to start with.

(If the weight gets too heavy for your grip strength, change to an alternate grip.) Hinge from the hips while keeping the back flat and the shoulders pulled back. Again, feel the stretch in the hamstring and use that as your guide for the range of movement. Pause, then return to the starting position.

The main errors in this exercise may come from allowing the shoulders to drop, the back to round and the hips to turn out. Mobilize the thoracic spine and practise thoracic extension to help with keeping your chest up and your back tight and flat as you hinge forwards, and pull your shoulders back. If the hips turn out and you cannot keep them square, some SMR work on the glutes, ITB and biceps femoris may help. Tightness in these areas, especially the biceps femoris, can prevent you from keeping your hips square. Stretching the biceps femoris may be needed as well. To do this, stand tall with one foot resting on a bench in front. Keep the leg and torso straight and hinge forwards, pushing the hips back and turning slightly in towards the leg on the bench. You should feel a nice stretch down the outside of your hamstrings. Hold for twenty to thirty seconds.

Single-Leg Squat

Basic Technique

The single-leg squat is the ultimate single-leg strength exercise. It requires strength and control in all planes of movement and great activation of the hip stabilizers. Develop the single-leg squat by first working on the eccentric part of the exercise. Stand in front of a bench or step-up box, lift one foot off the floor and slowly lower yourself down to the bench, then use both legs to stand back up. Use the same technique as for double-leg squats: keep the shoulders down and chest up, shift the weight to the heel as you start to lower down, keep the knee in line with the hip and ankle and keep your standing foot straight. Take about three to five seconds to lower down or pause at two to three points on the way down.

Reverse-pattern technique can be used to develop the concentric part of the single-leg squat. Start sitting down on the bench or box and set yourself by lifting one foot and placing the other one on the floor in line with your hip and pulled in so that your toes are under the knee. Lean forwards from the hips until your shoulders are over the mid-foot and lift your chest. Press your heel into the floor, squeeze your glute and push up to a standing position. Keep the knee in line with the hip and ankle and keep your chest up and shoulders down. Sit back down using both legs, and repeat.

Developing isometric strength at the lowest position you can reach with good posture will quickly help you to improve strength and technique. Lower as far as you can and hold for three to five seconds before standing back up. Gradually increase the depth at which you can hold the isometric contraction. To work on the whole pattern, put the two techniques together. Lower down until your glute lightly touches the bench, then stand straight back up.

Single-Leg Squat Variation

This is a cross between a single-leg squat and a lateral step-up and is a good way to load the single-leg squat when you get stronger. You need to use a box set to about the level of your knee.

Single-leg squats have a lot of benefits even if you cannot squat down to full depth. Although most exercises should be done through the full range of movement most of the time, there are exceptions and incidences in which limited range can be applicable and beneficial. Doing single-leg squats, even in a small range of movement, will improve balance and the activation of important stabilizers, as well as triggering high glute activation. Just start by standing on one leg and lowering down as far as you can for about five to six repetitions for each leg. Make sure you have weight on your heel and flex from

the ankle, knee and hip as you lower. Keep your chest up and do not let your back round, and concentrate on keeping your knee in line with your ankle and hip and your foot straight. For a good variation on the single-leg squat, stand on the edge of a step-up box and, as you descend, use the passive leg to maintain balance and lower below the step.

Errors and Correction

The main points to watch for occur at the foot, knee and hip. During the descent the foot can turn out, the knee collapse inwards and the hips rotate out. These dysfunctions can occur independently, all together or in some other combination and if they are left unchecked they can lead to injury, particularly at the knee.

Neurogenic tension in the lower leg, ITB, glute max and medius and adductors may be present, so it is worth doing some SMR on these areas first and working on the tender points. SMR for the foot can also help – roll a golf ball under your foot, paying particular attention to the outer part of the arch. The glutes and hamstrings are important for controlling valgus collapse (the knee collapsing inwards), so activate them with some clams and hip lifts, then get ready to try again. Stand on one leg and transfer your weight to your heel, then descend slowly as far as you can while flexing from the hips and pushing them back. Descend only as far as you can while still maintaining foot knee and hip alignment. Focus on keeping everything in line as you move up and down, and slowly increase the depth as you become more proficient.

Single-leg squat, start: stand tall with one foot held just off the floor and hold hands together under the chin. Keep your chest up, shift your weight to your heel and push your hips back as you start to descend.

Single-leg squat, continuation: descend as far as you can while maintaining a flat back and good alignment from ankle to knee to hip.

CHAPTER 7

VERTICAL AND HORIZONTAL PULLING

When it comes to training the upper body, rather than thinking about working on muscles or muscle groups, focus instead on getting strong in a few movements and spending some time on the stabilizers. Pulling movements are too often considered to be secondary to pushing movements such as the bench press; if anything, it should be the other way round. Doing plenty of pulling movements will help to keep your shoulders healthy and strengthen your back, shoulders, arms and, indeed, your whole body with the right movements.

Vertical Pulling

The main pulling exercise to work on is pull-ups or chins. There are a few variations and all are excellent exercises for developing great upper-body strength. If you struggle with pull-ups there are ways to develop the strength and technique needed to perform them well. These will be explained later. All versions strengthen the forearms, upper arms, shoulders, upper and middle back, latisimus dorsi, the core and the chest, in other words, the whole of the upper body and the hips. If you neglect this vital exercise, you will be missing out.

Neutral-Grip Pull-Ups
This is the easiest version of the pull-up. The neutral grip is holding the bars that stick straight out towards you about shoulder width apart, with palms facing each other.

Start hanging with the arms straight and the neck in line with the spine, keeping the arms pulled into the shoulder sockets. Do not hang from the shoulder joints. The legs can hang straight if you have the room to let them or you can flex the knees and lift your heels up behind. Start to move your shoulders down as you pull yourself up. Squeezing your glutes will generate more tension in the posterior

Neutral-grip pull-ups, start: the start position is at the top with your chest pulled in to your hands, shoulders kept down and shoulder blades pulled together.

Neutral-grip pull-ups: lift the heels up behind you and squeeze the glutes, then lower down until the arms are straight. Pull straight back up to the top and pause before repeating.

Supinated-grip pull-ups or chins: the action is the same as for the neutral-grip pull-ups, except that the shoulders are rotated so that the palms are facing you.

chain and help control swinging of the body. At the top pull your chest right up to the bar – do not stop at the chin – keep the shoulders down and retract your shoulder blades. Keep the neck in line with the spine and do not poke your chin out over the bar – this just stresses the neck and makes it harder to keep the right position at the top. Push your chest up to get a little thoracic extension while you pause for a second or two before controlling the descent. As soon as the arms are fully straight, pull back up.

Supinated-Grip Pull-Ups or Chins
Hold the bar with an underhand grip at about shoulder width. This grip creates more

tension in the biceps and forearms and for most people is slightly harder than the neutral grip. Start hanging with the arms straight and start to bring the shoulders down as you pull your chest up to the bar and keep your chin in. Lift the chest and pull the shoulder blades together as you pause, then start the descent. Keep the shoulders down but allow the shoulder blades to retract and move round your ribs on the way down. When your arms are fully straight, pull yourself straight back up.

Pronated-Grip Pull-Ups
This version is the hardest as the angle of pull for the lats and biceps is sub-optimal due to the external rotation and abduction of the

Pronated-grip pull-ups: hold the bar with hands about one and a half times shoulder width apart and palms facing away from you. Keep shoulders down and shoulder blades together at the top and straighten arms completely at the bottom before pulling back up.

shoulders. The grip is an overhand grip on the bar at about one and a half times shoulder width. Do not go too wide with the grip. The range of movement becomes smaller the wider you go, making it less productive and placing more stress on the rotator cuff muscles. Keep your shoulders down as you pull up and touch your chest to the bar. Lift the chest slightly to extend the thoracic spine and retract the shoulder blades. Lower back down under control and pull back up as soon as the arms straighten out.

Developing the Strength

If you cannot yet do pull-ups, the best way to work up to it is to use isometric and eccentric contractions to develop the strength needed. Use a neutral grip to start and stand on a bench or step-up box that enables you to hold on about half way up the movement with your arms bent. Hold tight and jump up to the top position. Hold for two to three seconds then lower back to the bench. Rest for ten to fifteen seconds then repeat for five reps. Rest for one to two minutes between sets and work up to three to five sets. You can gradually increase the time you hold the contraction up to ten seconds. If you do this, consider one ten-second hold as one set.

For eccentric pull-ups, stand on a lower bench or the floor and jump up to the top position. Lift your heels up behind and hold for a second, then lower down slowly for about three to five seconds until the arms are straight and stand back on the bench or floor. To combine isometric and eccentric work, jump up and hold the top position for three seconds then lower a quarter of the way keeping the shoulders down and chest up. Pause for three seconds then lower to half way and hold for three seconds, then lower to three-quarters of the way down and hold, then straighten the arms and rest. Wait for about sixty seconds then repeat for three to five times.

Weighted Pull-Ups

If you find body-weight pull-ups fairly easy and can comfortably control a ten-second eccentric while keeping good form, you could try adding extra weight using a weight belt. The weight used should be based on you being able to perform three to five repetitions with good technique – shoulders down, chest up to the bar and controlling the descent all the way down to straight arms.

Errors and Correction

The biggest mistake made when performing pull-ups is shrugging the shoulders at the top of the pull and not retracting the scapulars. This is usually due to a lack of strength in the rhomboids and trapezius. If you struggle to get into the right position at the top, you need to start by building some upper-back strength with the horizontal pulling movements. After this, you can start to work on your pull-ups with the isometric holds and eccentric work; eventually you will be doing full pull-ups with good technique.

Horizontal Pulling

Inverted Rows

Inverted rows are the opposite movement to press-ups and great for developing strength in the upper back and arms. This exercise can be done by lying under a secured bar or using some kind of suspension training system such as the TRX. While the grip on a bar is fixed, a suspension system gives the added benefit of being able to change grip width during the movement. It allows you to start with your hands close together, then move them apart as you pull and add rotation into the pull.

Inverted rows, start: as for pull-ups, the start is actually with the chest up at the bar and the arms flexed. Lower yourself down under control until the arms are straight and the knees, hips and shoulders are aligned.

Inverted rows, continuation: pull the chest up to the bar while keeping the body straight. Do not shrug the shoulders, but squeeze the shoulder blades together. Pause before lowering back down.

If using a bar, it should be made secure in a power cage or something similar and set at a height about level with your waist. Lie on the floor under the bar, which should be above your chest. Reach up and grab the bar with a pronated (overhand) grip about one and a half times shoulder width. Start with the knees bent to about ninety degrees and lift the hips off the floor. Keep the alignment between your shoulders, hips and knees and pull your chest up to the bar. Keep your neck in line with your spine at all times and touch the bar with the bottom of the sternum. At the top position your elbows should be held at roughly forty-five degrees from your sides, your shoulders down – no shrugging – and your scapulars squeezed together. Hold this top position for a second, then lower back down, allow-ing the scapulars to move apart and glide round your ribs.

To progress this exercise, simply straighten your legs. To progress it further, put your feet up on to a bench or box and eventually add a weight vest.

If this is too hard to start with, set the bar higher – say, chest height – stand up straight, and hold the bar with the same grip and with straight arms. Keeping your body straight, walk the feet forwards under the bar until you are leaning back at about forty-five degrees, then pull your chest up to the bar, squeezing the shoulder blades together and keeping the shoulders down. This will make it a lot easier as you will have less work to do against gravity at this angle. As you get stronger, lower the bar and follow the progressions explained above.

Inverted rows (easier version): the bar is set higher to make this exercise a bit easier. Simply lower the bar as you get stronger.

Using a suspension system for inverted rows is a great option, as extra dimensions can be added to the exercise and it is easy to use. As with the bar, start with the body at about forty-five degrees and move the feet forwards to make it harder. Eventually you will be holding your shoulders just off the floor in the starting position. The difference from the bar version starts right from the beginning, where your arms will be hanging straight at shoulder width. From here you can pull yourself up with a neutral grip (palms facing each other), a pronated grip (palms facing down), or a supinated grip (palms facing up), or you can start and finish with a combination of grip. For example, starting with a pronated grip and finishing with a supinated grip, or the other way round, is a great way to add rotation work to the shoulders and forearms.

Suspension-system inverted rows, pronated grip: great for adding shoulder rotation into the movement as well as allowing for some adduction/abduction. At the bottom you can have a supinated, neutral or pronated grip; here, the grip is pronated.

Suspension-system inverted rows, neutral grip: rotate the shoulders on the way up and finish with a different grip; here the grip is neutral.

Barbell/Dumbbell Rows

The barbell row or bent-over row is an exercise that is all too frequently performed poorly. You have to have good mobility through the hips and a very strong back to get into the right position to make it effective and worthwhile. If you cannot get into the correct position choose a different exercise until you have developed the necessary mobility and strength. The other big problem is that many people try to lift far too much weight. Do not let your ego get in the way; instead, concentrate on getting strong with good technique. If your technique is poor, you are doing a different exercise, failing to strengthen what you are supposed to be strengthening and placing excessive stress on certain areas. Done correctly, this exercise will strengthen the upper back, shoulders and arms, and demand stability through the torso, hips and legs.

Stand tall, holding a barbell in front of you against the thighs, with an overhand grip. Start as you would for a stiff-leg dead lift, bend the knees to about twenty degrees and push the hips back, hinging forwards, while keeping the chest up and back straight. Hinge forwards about sixty degrees from the hips, so that your chest is a little above parallel to the floor and hold this position with your chest out, shoulders pulled down and arms straight. This is the start position. Pull the bar up and touch it to the bottom of your chest, keeping the shoulders down and squeezing your shoulder blades together, then lower the bar under control back to the start position. The movement comes from the shoulder blades pulling together, the shoulders extending and the elbows flexing. Do not allow your shoulders to drop or your back to round and do not try to swing the weight up using the legs and hips – there are other exercises for that. This same exercise can also be done holding a dumbbell in each hand and, like the suspension rows, allows for different grips and rotation to be included in the movement.

Barbell rows, start position: the position of the spine is crucial in this exercise. Make sure the back is flat and the muscles tight and keep a bend in the knees, with weight back on the heels.

Barbell rows, continuation: keep the weight light enough that you can pull it right to your chest and hold it there for a second or two. Keep the shoulders down and retract the shoulder blades as much as possible.

Standing Cable Rows

Cable rows can be a great alternative to barbell rows as you do not have to bend forwards and hold a posture that many find very difficult to maintain. Another great benefit is that they can be done standing on your feet. Transferring forces from the ground through your feet, up your legs, through your torso and up to your shoulders and arms is essential for developing strength for sports and everyday tasks. Athletes competing in seated sports such as kayaking or rowing, who spend a lot of time training in a flexed spine position, can benefit from the strong spinal position that can be achieved with standing cable rows. If you are used to doing seated cable rows, give the standing version a go. It is much easier to keep the spine from flexing and will help prepare you for exercises such as squats and dead lifts. Remember, lifting weights with a flexed spine is not a good idea. The cable can be set low to the ground or anywhere up the cable column to about a foot above head height.

To row with the cable set at the floor you need to hold the bar with an overhand grip, stand with feet about shoulder width apart, bend your knees to about twenty degrees and lean forwards from the hips to about forty-five degrees. The cable line of pull should be perpendicular to the torso. Push your heels down and squeeze your glutes, lift your chest and keep your shoulders down and back tight as you pull the bar to your chest. Squeeze the shoulder blades together and do not allow the humeral head to glide forwards. As you lower the bar back to the start position, pull your shoulder blades apart and around the ribs.

Setting the cable at waist height means you have to adopt a more upright posture to keep the cable perpendicular to the chest and, as you use more weight, you will have to

Standing cable rows, start position: with the cable set at the floor, angle the torso so that it is perpendicular to the chest.

Standing cable rows, continuation: maintain your torso position as you pull the cable right to your chest and fully retract the shoulder blades.

stand in a deeper squat position to counter the forward pull of the cable. With a heavy weight the starting posture will be almost a deep squat position, with the hips pushed back a bit more and the feet gripping the floor hard.

The overhead cable position is slightly different in that the line of pull is not perpendicular to the torso, but half way between a horizontal and a vertical pull. The angle can be varied slightly as long as it is above the head and slightly in front at about a hundred and forty degrees. This is also a good exercise with which to use a supinated grip. Hold the bar at about shoulder width, step back from the cable a couple of feet and lower down to a squat position, with the thighs about parallel to the floor and arms straight. Keep the torso vertical and lift the chest to extend the thoracic spine slightly, and pull the cable bar down towards your chest. Squeeze the shoulder blades together and pull the shoulders down. Hold here for a second then straighten your arms under control. The return part of the movement is great for getting some upward rotation of the scapulars (shoulder blades) –think about pulling your scapulars out and round your ribs.

Bench Dumbbell Rows

This is a great exercise for working on horizontal pull. It is a good way to focus more on the upper back, if this is needed, as it eliminates the need to concentrate so much on postural control. Lie prone on a bench set at a small incline with your head off the end, so that your chin is free and you can keep your neck in line with your spine. The feet should be on the floor on either side on the bench. Hold a dumbbell in each hand and pull them up to the sides of the bench, squeezing the shoulder blades together and keeping the shoulders down and the chest on the bench.

Bench dumbbell rows, start position: do not incline the bench too much as this will shift focus to the upper traps. Keep the chest down on the bench and the neck in line with the spine.

Bench dumbbell rows, continuation: do not let the shoulders shrug or humerus glide forwards as you pull the dumbbells up and squeeze the shoulder blades together.

Dumbbell one-arm rows, start position: support your weight with one hand and knee on the bench and keep alignment from the ear through the shoulders to the hips.

Split-stance cable one-arm rows, start position: stand with feet about twice shoulder width apart and hold the cable at chest height in the hand opposite to the front leg, with a straight arm.

Dumbbell one-arm rows, continuation: pull the dumbbell up to your side moving the scapular towards your spine without moving the humeral head forward.

Split-stance cable one-arm rows, continuation: keep the torso still as you pull the cable to the side of your chest. Move the scapular in and keep the shoulders down and your neck in line with your spine.

Single-Arm Rows

One-arm rows are often under-rated, but they are good exercises for learning how to control rotation of the spine and activating the obliques as well as strengthening the back, shoulders and arms. All single-arm pulling movements activate the contra lateral stabilizers of the torso, such as the quadratus lumborum, the internal and external obliques and right down through the opposite hip and leg.

Dumbbell One-Arm Rows

Start by standing a couple of feet in front of a bench with feet about twice shoulder width apart, bend forwards at the hips and support yourself with one hand on the bench. Bend your knees and keep your back straight to pick a dumbbell off the floor with your free hand. Keep your neck in line with your spine and keep your back straight and tight as you pull the dumbbell up to your side. Prevent rotation of the torso by bracing your abdominals and pull the scapular in towards your spine. Do not shrug the shoulders or let the humerus glide forwards.

This exercise can also be done with one knee and hand resting on the bench. Stand next to a bench and place the inside knee and the same-side hand on to the bench to support yourself. Place your standing leg out to the side until your pelvis is square to the floor. Keep your back flat and do not rotate the torso or shoulders as you pull the dumbbell up to your side.

Split-Stance Cable One-Arm Rows

Set the cable at about chest height, stand tall with the cable in your right hand and step back a couple of feet to lift the weight stack. Take a step back with your right foot, about twice shoulder width in length. Keep the front foot, the left one, flat on the floor, stay on the toes of the rear foot and keep the knees slightly bent. Keep the heel of the front foot pressed into the floor and squeeze your glute as you pull the cable in towards your side. The hips should remain square and the torso straight, with chest up and no shrugging of the shoulders. As with all the single-arm row movements, do not allow the head of the humerus to glide forwards. Keep it back and pull the shoulder blade in towards the spine. Prevent any rotation of the hips and torso by bracing the abdominals as much as is needed, without over-bracing.

CHAPTER 8

VERTICAL AND HORIZONTAL PUSHING

Pushing, pulling and leg strength are the cornerstones of strength training. Most people seem to be fairly familiar with horizontal pushing – indeed, they usually do too much of it – so drag yourself away from the bench press for a while and stand on your feet to do some pressing. You may find you have a few mobility issues to work on.

Vertical Pushing

Standing Barbell Press

One of the best-known and most frequently used strength exercises is the standing barbell press. It has been used as a measure of strength for centuries and is still a great whole-body exercise for developing strength. Stand up straight with the feet shoulder width apart and hold a bar with an overhand shoulder-width grip resting across the anterior deltoids. The movement starts at the ground; follow the advice of Pavel Tsatsouline and Stuart McGill, who use the technique of muscle tension to trigger a wave of neural firing that increases strength. Grip the floor with your feet, keep your legs straight and tense your thighs, glutes and abdominals, then press the bar up over your head until the arms are straight and the elbows are locked out. As you start the press you will have to pull your chin in and lift your chest slightly to move back so that the bar can travel straight up. The bar should be straight overhead with the neck in line with the spine, the arms level with the ears and everything

Barbell standing press, start position: stand up straight with the barbell held in front, just below the chin, with a grip just wider than the shoulders.

Barbell standing press, continuation: squeeze glutes and abdominals as you press the bar overhead and straighten the arms in line with the ears.

aligned from the shoulders through the hips to the ankles. Lower the bar under control back to the front of the shoulders.

Errors and Correction

The problems associated with this exercise come mainly from immobility around the shoulders and upper back. If you are too tight in the thoracic spine and shoulders you will end up leaning back too much, arching the back or pressing the weight forward of the midline, and usually both. Inefficient movement caused by immobility leads to fatigue and loss of strength,

as well as excessive loading on structures such as the spine. You need to be able to maintain a neutral pelvis and keep your back in a strong and stable position, without an excessive arch in the lumbar spine and without leaning backwards. Do some SMR work on the lats, chest and upper back and then work on thoracic mobility and activation of the serratus anterior and trapezius. This should help improve your movement over time. If you cannot press a barbell with proper technique, use the single-arm press until you have developed the necessary mobility.

Standing Dumbbell Press

This is pretty much the same as the barbell press with the dumbbells allowing for a variation in grip and rotation during the press and return. Start in the same standing position, holding the dumbbells at the shoulders with a neutral grip, palms facing each other, tense legs, glutes and abs, then press the dumbbells

Barbell standing press (poor technique): if you have to lean back and arch your spine to get your arms straight up, you should not perform this lift until you have improved your mobility.

Standing dumbbell press, start: this is essentially the same as the barbell press, except that the dumbbells allow for a varied grip and shoulder rotation. The grip here is neutral but a pronated grip could be used.

Standing dumbbell press, continuation: keep glutes and abdominals tight as you press the dumbbells straight up.

Single-arm press, start: stand straight holding a dumbbell at the shoulder with the elbow in close to the side. Keep the chest up and extend the other arm slightly by your side.

up and rotate the palms inwards to finish standing straight with palms facing forwards.

Single-Arm Press

The single-arm press is easier to perform with good technique than the barbell or dumbbell press. This means that most people can use it to develop pressing strength while they are working on the mobility required for the barbell press. Besides this, it is a great exercise in its own right for developing strength and stability, as pressing one-arm overhead improves contra-lateral activation of the obliques and quadratus lumborum among others.

Start standing straight as for the barbell press, holding a dumbbell in one hand at the shoulder. Grip the floor with your feet and tense the legs, glutes, abs and the free hand at your side. Do not over-tense, though – you should be able to maintain breathing. Take a breath and hold it as

Single-arm press, continuation: brace the abdominals and squeeze the glutes as you drive the dumbbell up and bring it in line with your ear.

you press the dumbbell, then maintain tension through your torso as you take a breath at the top then hold on the way down. While pressing the dumbbell, keep the free hand tense and the arm slightly extended by your side, to help to stabilize the flexing shoulder. Lock out the arm over the head in line with your ear, then lower under control.

To add rotation, start with a neutral grip and rotate internally as you press the dumbbell, finishing with the palm facing forwards at the top, then rotate back to neutral on the way down.

Horizontal Pushing

Press-Ups

Probably the best but most under-rated horizontal pressing movement is the press-up. There are loads of press-up versions to keep you challenged and they can be done anywhere without the need for equipment. The trouble is, doing them properly is much harder than most people imagine. The press-up is a whole-body exercise that starts off as a hand plank, which in itself is a great core-strengthening exercise demanding isometric strength through the legs, hips, trunk, shoulders and arms. As the body is lowered towards the floor the chest, shoulders and arms contract eccentrically, then an isometric contraction stops you hitting the floor and a concentric contraction pushes you back up. There are also isometric contractions from the lats to help stabilize the trunk, especially on the way back up, as well as involvement from the upper back, rhomboids, trapezius and from the serratus anterior to control scapular movement.

Once you have become stronger at press-ups, they may also be used as part of the warm-up and activation for the main part of the training session. There is a significant amount of benefit to be gained from properly performed press-ups.

Press-Up Technique

Start in the hand plank position, supporting your body on your toes and hands. Your arms should be straight, and hands about one and a half times shoulder width apart, and in line with the shoulders. As you lower towards the floor, keep your legs straight and your pelvis in

Press-ups, start: start with the body held straight and hands just wider than and in line with the shoulders.

Press-ups, continuation: tense the glutes a little and keep the whole body aligned as you lower to the floor. Bring the shoulder blades together and keep the elbows pointing back about forty-five degrees. Press back up, pulling the shoulder blades apart.

neutral, trying to maintain the shallow curves of the spine and pointing the elbows back so that they are about forty-five degrees away from your sides. Bring your scapulars (shoulder blades) together as you reach the bottom position of just above the floor. Do not shrug your shoulders or allow the humeral head to glide forwards; keeping your shoulders down and retracting your scapulars should prevent this from happening. Forward glide of the humeral head can cause damage to the anterior connective tissues and lead to further shoulder problems. Keep your body straight as you push yourself back up to the start position. When your arms are straight, do not stop, but push up a bit more and pull your scapulars around your ribs. This will activate your serratus anterior, which are involved in scapular upward rotation and essential to optimal shoulder function and health.

Errors and Correction

The most common problems experienced with press-ups are due to a lack of stability and isometric strength through the hips, trunk and shoulders. As you start to flex your arms and lower your body towards the floor, you need to guard against poking your chin out, dropping your hips and shrugging your shoulders.

To develop the correct technique the best approach is to make the exercise easier and practise the movement in this way, to groove the pattern and work on core strength with planks and plank variations. To make it easier, elevate your hands on to the edge of a bench, box or bar racked at the required height in a power cage, or anything else at the right height.

Start with something set about waist height and rest your hands against it with your arms straight. Walk the feet back a little and lower the hips until you have alignment from the ankles through to the shoulders. Keep your body straight and lower your chest to the bar; remember to keep your shoulders down and pull your shoulder blades together. Brace your abdominals a bit more and squeeze your glutes as you start to push back up. This should help to keep your torso stiff and prevent your back from sagging. Another thing that contributes to the back arching is a

Press-up (poor technique): if your press-ups look like this, stop doing them and elevate your hands to make them easier until you have good technique.

forward tilt in the pelvis. Practise pelvic positioning while standing and loosen up the hip flexors and strengthen up the glutes. Work on press-ups in this position until the technique is perfect and you can perform them comfortably, then lower the hands a bit more and build strength until you are performing them with your hands on the floor.

Press-Up Progressions

Elevated-Feet Press-Ups

The easiest way to progress the press-up is to raise the feet. Start with a small lift and raise the feet higher as your strength increases. An added advantage of elevating the feet is that the serratus anterior is activated to a greater

Elevated-feet press-ups: a good way to progress your press-ups as it activates your serratus anterior more, as long as you move your shoulder blades in and out.

Elevated-feet press-ups: maintain alignment throughout and keep the elbows in and shoulders down.

extent, as long as you push all the way up and pull the shoulder blades around the ribs. If your wrists cause you some discomfort try using some press-up handles, which will allow you to keep your wrists straight. Just remember not to lower too close to the floor, which may allow your humeral head to push forwards. Keep your shoulders down and pull your shoulder blades together.

Another great way to make your press-ups or any other body-weight exercise harder is to use a weight vest. The weight on it can be adjusted as you get stronger.

Press-Ups on One Leg

Start in the normal press-up position and lift one foot off the floor a few inches. Keep the leg straight and use the glute to maintain the

Press-ups on one leg: the body position and action are the same as for regular press-ups, except that you lift one foot off the floor.

Press-ups on one leg: keep the foot elevated throughout the total number of reps or alternate legs with each rep.

leg lift. Lifting one foot will shift your body weight from four points of support to three, thus increasing the load on the three points. The load will also shift slightly to the shoulder opposite the elevated foot, so make sure to do the same number of repetitions with each foot off the floor. To make this one harder, try bringing the knee of the elevated foot up and out to the same-side elbow as you lower to the floor.

Press-Ups with Arm Lift

This will require stability and anti-rotation through the torso as well as shoulder stability, mobility and strength. Start as you would for a normal press-up and, as you push back up from the low position, keep your body straight and lift one arm up and out to the side slightly, with the thumb pointing up. Hold this position for two to three seconds then

Press-ups with arm lift: the action is the same as for the normal press-up, except that, as you press up from the bottom, you lift one arm up and out at an angle. Lift it as high as you can and point the thumb up. Keep the body straight and do not rotate the hips or torso.

143

Elbow to knee press-ups: as you lower your body to the floor, bring one knee up and out to the side towards your elbow.

return the hand to the floor. Do another full press-up and lift the other arm as you reach the top, then repeat with alternating arms for a number of repetitions.

Elbow to Knee Press-Ups

Start in the normal press-up position. As you lower to the floor, bring one knee out to the side and up to the same-side elbow, then press back up while simultaneously returning

the leg to the start position. Then repeat the press-up while bringing the other knee up to the other elbow. Keep alternating the knees with each press-up.

Medicine-Ball Press-Ups

Medicine balls are great for doing all kinds of variations and here are a couple to get you thinking. To change the emphasis of the movement quite a bit and target the triceps

Medicine-ball press-ups: to hit the arms and shoulders more, place both hands on a medicine ball directly under the chest, with arms straight.

Medicine-ball press-ups: keep the body aligned and elbows in by your sides as you lower your chest to the ball.

more, start with both hands on the medicine ball directly under your chest, with your arms straight. Simply lower your chest to the medicine ball, keeping your body straight, shoulders down and elbows in by your sides. Elevating the feet will make this harder.

Medicine-Ball Roll Press-Ups

Try press-ups with one hand on a medicine ball and one hand on the floor, then, as you push up, roll the medicine ball across to the other hand and repeat. Another option is to do a press-up from the bottom and balance on to one hand on top of the medicine ball for a second or two, then repeat for a number of repetitions.

Medicine-ball roll press-ups: start in the press-up position with the hands slightly wider than the shoulders and one hand on a medicine ball. Keep the body aligned and shoulders down as you lower towards the ground.

Medicine-ball roll press-ups: keep the elbows pointing back, at forty-five degrees, and stop with the chest just above the level of the medicine ball. Press back up, roll the ball over to the other hand and repeat.

Suspension-System Press-Ups

As with pulling exercises, suspension systems are a great addition to a strength programme and offer some challenging variations. Start easy with this one and give yourself time to get the feel and control of the handles. To make it easier, stand taller to use a small forward lean. To make it tougher, just lower the handles closer to the floor and eventually elevate your feet to make it even harder. Remember all the major points: body straight, neutral spine and pelvis, shoulders down, elbows pointing slightly back, and shoulder blades moving together on the way down and pushed apart on the way up. For an extra movement, a suspension system allows you to bring your hands together at the top and move them out as you lower down. You can also turn your hands in so that the palms are facing at the top, then rotate them out so the palms face backwards at the bottom to get some rotation, adduction and abduction of the shoulders.

Suspension-system press-ups, start position: suspension systems allow you to include rotation, adduction and abduction options into your press-ups. Start with hands together using a pronated grip.

Suspension-system press-ups, continuation: keep the body straight and move the arms out to the sides as you lower down and turn the palms to a neutral grip. Alternatively, start with palms facing and turn to a pronated grip as you descend.

One-Arm Press-Ups

One-arm press-ups demand not only stability and strength through the shoulder and arm, but also anti-rotation strength through the torso. Most people will find one-arm press-ups extremely challenging and because of this there is a progression to follow. It is important to make sure you have good control around the shoulder and scapular when you perform these progressions, to develop correct movement patterns. For this reason, you should start with the easiest version and concentrate on getting a good feel for the movement. The first stage is to use a wall. Stand up straight an arm's length from the wall, with feet shoulder width apart and one arm extended at shoulder height with the hand on the wall. Keep your chest and hips square to the wall as you bend your arm and lower towards the wall.

Keep your shoulder down and your elbow in to about forty-five degrees from your side and pull the scapular across to your spine. Keep your body straight and pull your scapular out around your ribs as you press back up.

When you can comfortably perform ten repetitions like this with perfect form, you are ready to make it harder. Set a bar just below chest height and stand with one arm behind your back and the other held straight, supporting yourself on the bar. Now lower yourself to the bar in the same way as above. The bottom of your chest should be parallel to the bar at the bottom of the movement, with the shoulder held down, elbow in and scapular pulled across to the spine and flat against your back.

To progress further, simply lower the bar until eventually you are able to do the press-ups off the floor.

One-arm press-ups, start: to develop the technique and strength for this movement, start with a bar set at about chest height.

One-arm press-ups, continuation: lower the chest towards the bar and do not allow the body to twist, keep the elbow pointing back forty five degrees and the shoulders down.

One-arm press-ups, progression: eventually you may be able to do one-arm press-ups off the floor. Place one arm behind your back and your feet slightly wider than shoulder width.

One-arm press-ups, finish: lower down as far as you can, keeping as straight as you can, then press back up.

Dumbbell Chest Press

The next obvious horizontal pushing exercise would be the bench press, for which you can use a barbell. However, dumbbells offer more variations and provide a greater challenge to stabilizers. Start lying supine on a bench, making sure you have five points of contact: head, upper back and hips on the bench and feet flat on the floor. Do not lift your feet as you do your presses. You need your feet in contact with the floor for stability and to push into the ground, activating the posterior chain, when pressing the weight. The spine should also have its natural curves when lying on a bench, and lifting the feet and legs in the air can posteriorly tilt the pelvis and flatten the spine, as well as make you unstable. Hold a dumbbell in each hand – get someone to hand them to you if they are heavy – and start to lower them down and out to the sides of your chest slightly. The bottom position should be the same as the bottom position of the press-up. The elbows should be about forty-five degrees out to the sides of

your chest, the forearms perpendicular to the floor and the dumbbells level with the bottom of your sternum.

Maintain all five points of contact and do not let your shoulders shrug up or your back arch up excessively off the bench. Think about pulling the weight down and moving the scapulars together, then pull the scapulars apart as you press the weight back up. Do not lower the dumbbells too far, just low enough that the handles of the dumbbells are just above the level of the chest. The other thing to watch for is humeral glide, when the head of the humerus rotates and slides forwards, pressing into the anterior joint capsule of the shoulder. This is something to be avoided as it will stretch the joint capsule and anterior ligaments and eventually lead to all kinds of shoulder problems. It will also groove poor movement patterns for the humerus and scapular.

One of the advantages of dumbbells is that you can rotate them, move them in and out and use different grip positions. Try starting

Dumbbell chest press, start: keep the feet on the floor and hips, upper back and head on the bench. Hold the dumbbells above the chest with palms facing.

Dumbbell chest press, continuation: keep a small arch in your lower back and shoulders down as you lower the dumbbells and rotate them out.

with a neutral grip (palms facing) and dumbbells together at the top of the movement then move them out and rotate them internally (turn the palms towards your feet) as you lower them. This will add rotation, abduction and adduction, making it a tri-planar exercise.

Incline Dumbbell Chest Press

The incline press provides an angle between the horizontal and vertical presses. Adjust the bench to about forty-five degrees up from horizontal and lie supine with the five points of contact in place. Start with the arms

One-arm dumbbell chest press, start: keep the feet on the floor and a small arch in the lower back. Hold the dumbbell with a straight arm, placing your free hand on your hip.

One-arm dumbbell chest press, continuation: lower the dumbbell to the side of your chest and keep the elbow in by your side. Squeeze glutes and push feet into the floor as you press the weight.

straight and perpendicular to the floor, lower under control in the same way as for the flat chest press, then press back up. Again, do not lower too far – just above the chest is fine for most people – and keep the shoulders down at the bottom of the movement to prevent humeral glide. Rotation can be used here in the same way as for the flat press.

One-Arm Dumbbell Chest Press

The one-arm chest press is a great exercise for getting a feel for how important the whole body is for transferring forces. The asymmetrical weight needs to be countered by bracing the abdominals and pushing your feet, especially the same-side foot, into the floor and activating your glutes to stabilize your body and transfer the forces through to your lifting arm. Lie supine on a bench as you would for the normal dumbbell chest press, with feet on the floor and glutes, upper back and head touching the bench. Hold a dumbbell in one hand with the arm straight and perpendicular to the floor and place the other hand on your hip. Maintain the small arch in your lower back as you lower the dumbbell, keeping your elbow in close to your side and your shoulders down. Stop with the dumbbell just above the level of your chest. Move your shoulder blade in towards your spine and do not let your humeral head push too far forward. Then press the dumbbell back to the start position, moving your shoulder blade out as you do.

One-Arm Dumbbell Chest Press (Advanced)

The one-arm dumbbell chest press can be made more challenging for the whole body by moving your shoulders to the edge of the bench. This position will force you to use your glutes, back and abdominals to hold a stable position while you press the weight. Sit on the floor, side on to a bench, with your knees bent to forty-five degrees, feet on the floor and upper back resting against the bench. Hold a dumbbell at your waist and lift your hips off the floor so that you have alignment from your knees through your hips to your shoulders and head, which are resting on the bench and ninety degrees at your knees. Lift the dumbbell with both hands until the arms are straight then put one hand on your hip while holding the dumbbell in the other hand with the arm straight. Lower the dumbbell down to the side of your chest, keeping the elbow in by your side and protracting the shoulder blade. Do not lower the dumbbell too far or allow your humeral head to lift up and push forwards. Push your heels into the floor, squeeze your glutes and keep your hips in line with your knees and shoulders as you press the dumbbell up to the start position.

One-arm dumbbell chest press (advanced), start: make sure the head and shoulders are supported on the bench and keep the knees, hips and shoulders aligned.

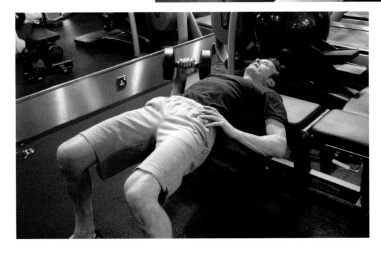

One-arm dumbbell chest press (advanced), continuation: keep the heels on the floor and squeeze the glutes to maintain stability and prevent movement of the torso.

CHAPTER 9

PLANNING TRAINING

At The Beginning

Knowing where to start and what programme to follow can be difficult if you have not weight trained before. The truth is, if you are a complete beginner to this kind of training, you will see strength gains with almost any programme, but that does not mean you should follow any old schedule of exercises. The most important thing is to keep it simple. Get into good habits from the very start and spend some time developing technique with the big lifts and establishing a sound base of mobility and stability. Start out with a good programme and you are less likely to develop muscle imbalances and injuries as you progress.

At the beginning your body will respond well and make fast gains, but this will not last. When you start out your nervous system is not used to having to activate all those muscle fibres and coordinate all those movements – in other words, you are not operating at anywhere near your potential. In the first few weeks or even months, you will be developing skills, firing up your nervous system and getting your muscles, tendons, bones, joints, indeed, your whole body, used to lifting progressively heavier loads. After a few weeks, you will be working closer to your potential and the strength increases will slow down. Strength is relative to each individual so it is important to remember that you are just trying to get stronger than you were, not stronger than your neighbour or colleague. Any increase in strength is going to be a benefit to you.

Preparation

The first stage is to prepare you for the training session, using one of the following sample warm-up routines. When you have become accustomed to these, have a look at the exercises in Chapters 2 and 4 and try putting together some of your own routines.

The first routine is an introduction to preparation work and contains SMR to target the main problem areas experienced by most people, along with a few mobility activities to get you moving. Use body-weight movements for the specific activation and make the press-ups and inverted rows easier than your working sets by raising the hands. Take your time to get familiar with the different techniques and concentrate on developing good movement with just a few drills.

The second routine has more SMR work, some more movement preparation and slightly harder activation movements.

The third routine is a more advanced one and includes more of every element. By the time you use this one, or a similar one, you should be well practised in most of the techniques and movements. You should be able to move through them all quickly and seamlessly in ten to fifteen minutes. As you become more familiar with SMR work and experience less tenderness, you can reduce the amount of time you spend on SMR – ten to fifteen seconds on less painful areas and a bit longer (around 30 seconds) on any sore spots. The mobility and activation sections become more integrated and the exercises harder.

PREPARATION/WARM-UP ROUTINE ONE

Exercise	Reps	Sets
SMR (thighs and hips): piriformis, glute med, TFL, ITB		
	10–15	1
Mobility/movement prep: ankle mobility 1, thoracic mobility 1, hip mobility 3, hip mobility 1		
	8-10	1
Combination 2	8–10	1
Activation: bridge lifts, prone W to Y; plank, side plank (10'–30')		
	8–10	2
Specific activation: BW squats, BW SLDL, press-ups (easy) and inverted rows (easy)		
	5–10	1

PREPARATION/WARM-UP ROUTINE TWO

Exercise	Reps	Sets
SMR: calf, piriformis, glute med, TFL, ITB, adductors, rotator cuff		
	10–15	1
Mobility/movement prep: ankle mobility 2, thoracic mobility 2, hip mobility 3, hip mobility 1		
	8–10	1
Combination 1 and 2		
	10 each	1
Activation: single-leg bridge lifts, kneeling W to Y, hand plank with alternate knees, hand plank with alternate leg lifts		
	8–10	1–2
Specific activation: goblet squats (light weight), SLDL (light weight), press-ups, inverted rows		
	8 each	1–2

PREPARATION/WARM-UP ROUTINE THREE

Exercise	Reps	Sets
SMR: calf, piriformis, glute med, TFL, ITB, adductors, lats, pecs, rotator cuff, thoracic		
	10'–30'	1
Mobility/movement prep: ankle mobility 1, thoracic mobility 1, hip mobility 4, hip mobility 2		
	8–10	1
Combination 3, squat mobility, judo press-ups		
	8–10	1
Activation: single-leg hip lifts, monster side walks, band Ls, ball saw		
	8–10	1–2
Specific activation: one to two circuits of the exercises to be used in the main part of the workout with light weights		
	8–10	1–2

A Simple Programme

If you are new to weight training, try following this simple programme for four to six weeks. It will help you to develop important movement skills that you will need later on. Goblet squats are great for learning good squat technique, stiff-leg dead lifts will get you perfecting the hip hinge, inverted rows and press-ups will groove scapular retraction and protraction and stability ball roll-outs will train your abdominal region to control spinal extension.

Exercise	Sets	Reps
Goblet squats	3–5	5–8
SLDL	3–5	5–8
Inverted rows	3–5	5–10
Press-ups	3–5	5–10
Stability ball roll-outs		
	3–5	5–10

Do these exercises in a circuit format going through them all with about thirty seconds' rest between exercises and around one to two minutes' rest between each circuit. Alternatively, split it in two and complete the goblet squats and SLDLs as a pair with around thirty seconds' rest between the exercises and one to two minutes' rest between pairs, then complete the remaining three exercises in the same manner. These methods can be used alone or alternated between workouts or weeks and both are effective and time-efficient ways to complete a strength-training session.

A More Advanced Programme

When you have established good technique and improved your strength and work capacity you can move to a more advanced programme. Again, keep it simple with a tried and tested programme such as the five by five. The exercises and structure of the training sessions can be changed but the basic premise remains the same. Stick with three to five big movements and do five sets of five repetitions for each one. To keep the session times under an hour, split the exercises into two sections as before. Complete one set of squats, rest thirty to sixty seconds, then complete one set of pull-ups, rest for sixty seconds, then repeat for five rounds. Do the same with the SLDLs, overhead presses and roll-outs. As always, good technique must be maintained for all exercises and the weight increased only when you can complete all the exercises for all sets with that good technique.

This structure works well if you intend to train twice a week. However, if you can train three or four times a week, you can split it into two sessions and just keep alternating them. The split sessions will be shorter and this can allow you to spend a little more time in each session on mobility and stability exercises, or add another exercise or two.

When training to increase strength you need to stick to the same exercises for a few weeks to allow for adaptation. If you change them too often it will make it difficult to show progression. On the other hand, if you stay too long with the same routine you will stagnate and eventually start to go backwards. There are a couple of simple ways to avoid this. Every three to four weeks, build in a de-loading week during which you reduce the training intensity and volume. Instead of five sets, reduce to three and use about seventy-five per cent of the weight you were using. This will be enough to prevent you losing the strength gains but allow your body to recover and adapt to the training stimulus. After the de-load week change the exercises and complete another three- to four-week block. This can be a good time to introduce some single-leg and single-arm pressing and pulling movements.

When your movement and technique are good, you can increase the weight you are lifting a little each week, always ensuring that your technique remains correct. Use small increments in weight and keep a record of the weights used, and sets and reps completed at each session. Refer back to the main text for technical information and advice on how to develop good movement. Do not be in a hurry; take your time to build the strength and allow for sufficient recovery and adaptation.

The exercises within the following sample training blocks are a guide and can be changed to suit your particular requirements or ability.

TWICE A WEEK TRAINING PLAN (FIRST BLOCK)

Exercise	Sets	Reps
Back or front squats	5	5
Neutral-grip pull-ups	5	5
SLDLs	5	5
Standing barbell press	5	5
Bar roll-outs	5	5

TWICE A WEEK TRAINING PLAN (SECOND BLOCK)

Exercise	Sets	Reps
Olympic bar dead lifts	5	5
Supinated-grip pull-ups	5	5
DB lunge walk	5	5
Single-arm press	5	5 each
Pallof press	5	10 each side

THREE OR FOUR SESSIONS A WEEK TRAINING PLAN (FIRST BLOCK)

Day One

Exercise	Sets	Reps
Back squats	5	5
Neutral-grip pull-ups	5	5
Standing barbell press	5	5
Pallof press	5	10 each side

Day Two

Exercise	Sets	Reps
SLDLs	5	5
Dumbbell bench rows	5	5
Dumbbell chest press	5	5
Bar roll-outs	5	5

THREE OR FOUR SESSIONS A WEEK TRAINING PLAN (SECOND BLOCK)

Day One

Exercise	Sets	Reps
Olympic bar dead lifts	5	5
Pronated-grip pull-ups	5	5
Single-arm press	5	5
Pallof press with rotation	5	8–10 each side

Day Two

Exercise	Sets	Reps
RFESS	5	5 each
DB one-arm rows	5	5 each
One-arm DB chest press	5	5 each
Stir the Pot	5	10-20

Techniques

When you have been training for a few months and have significantly increased your strength, there are a couple of effective strength-training methods that you might like to try.

Clusters

The cluster method allows you to lift heavy weights and reach the high-threshold motor units without going into severe neural fatigue or compromising technique. Cluster training works best with the big movements such as dead lifts, squats and pull-ups, but it is also good for developing single-leg squat strength. First, you need to select a weight that is equivalent to around ninety to ninety-five per cent of your IRM (one repetition maximum). This can be roughly calculated from the five repetition weights with which you have been training. There have been several tables devised to help with this calculation, but there is a degree of inaccuracy and you could end up with too much weight on the bar. It may be better simply to add ten per cent to your five-repetition weight. This will give you something close to your required weight and, if you complete your clusters easily, you can just add a little more weight. Clusters are used frequently with Olympic lifting techniques and there are different applications depending on the training goal. In this instance, they are used to increase strength.

Very simply, clusters are a set of three to five single repetitions with a brief rest between each repetition. Using squats as an example, you do one repetition, return the bar to the rack, rest for ten to twenty seconds, then get back under the bar and complete another repetition. Repeat this for three to five repetitions, rest for two to three minutes, then complete another set. Try to work up to three sets of three to five repetitions. Clusters induce a strong neural stimulus so the

157

method should not be used for more than two exercises in a session and two sessions a week. Make sure the technique is good for every repetition and try to maintain the same tempo for each one. If the speed significantly decreases – say, during your fourth repetition – then stop the set there, otherwise the technique will suffer. There is a good chance you will not get the fifth repetition at all and you will also risk going into neural fatigue.

Wave Loading

The wave-loading method can be used to increase work capacity and strength and to take advantage of post-activation potentiation (PAP). This is a state of enhanced neural activation following a heavy loaded exercise, which helps increase potential strength for a following exercise. There are many variations of wave loading and this example is simple and effective. Three sets of an exercise create a wave and you complete usually two and a maximum of three waves.

Using dead lifts as an example, you do five repetitions with your five-repetition weight, then add around five per cent more weight, rest one to two minutes, perform three repetitions, then add another five per cent of your five-rep weight, rest one to two minutes, then perform one repetition. That is the first wave completed. Rest two to three minutes and start again at five repetitions with a little extra weight for each set.

EXAMPLE WAVE LOADING

Exercise	Weight	Reps	Rest
Dead lift – Wave One	100kg	5	1–2 mins
	105kg	3	1–2 mins
	110kg	1	2–3 mins
Dead lift – Wave Two	105kg	5	1–2 mins
	110kg	3	1–2 mins
	115kg	1	2–3 mins

Once you have increased your strength with a couple of cycles of straight sets using five by five, give these methods a go. Try using wave loading for a three- to four-week block, then use cluster training for a three- to four-week block, then return to five by five for another block. As long as you keep varying your training methods you will avoid pattern overload and keep the training stimulating. Just remember not to change it every couple of sessions, but allow enough time for improvement. Wave loading and clusters should be reserved for the big strength movements and no more than two exercises in each training session.

BIBLIOGRAPHY

Beachle, Thomas R. and Earle, Roger W. Editors 3rd Edition. *Essentials of Strength Training and Conditioning* (National Strength and Conditioning Association 2008)

Boyle, Michael. *Advances in Functional Training* (On Target Publications 2010)

Cook, Gray. *Movement* (On Target Publications 2010)

McGill, Stuart. 4th Edition. *Ultimate Back Fitness and Performance* (Backfitpro Inc. 2009)

McGill, Stuart. 2nd Edition. *Low Back Disorders : evidence-based prevention and rehabilitation* (Human Kinetics 2007)

Myers, Thomas W. 2nd Edition. *Anatomy Trains* (Churchill Livingstone 2009)

Sahrmann, Shirley A. *Diagnosis and Treatment of Movement Impairment Syndromes* (Mosby 2002)

Siff, Mel C. *Supertraining* 6th Edition (2003)

Zatsiorsky, Vladimir M. and Kraemer, William J. 2nd Edition. *Science and Practice of Strength Training* (Human Kinetics 2006)

INDEX